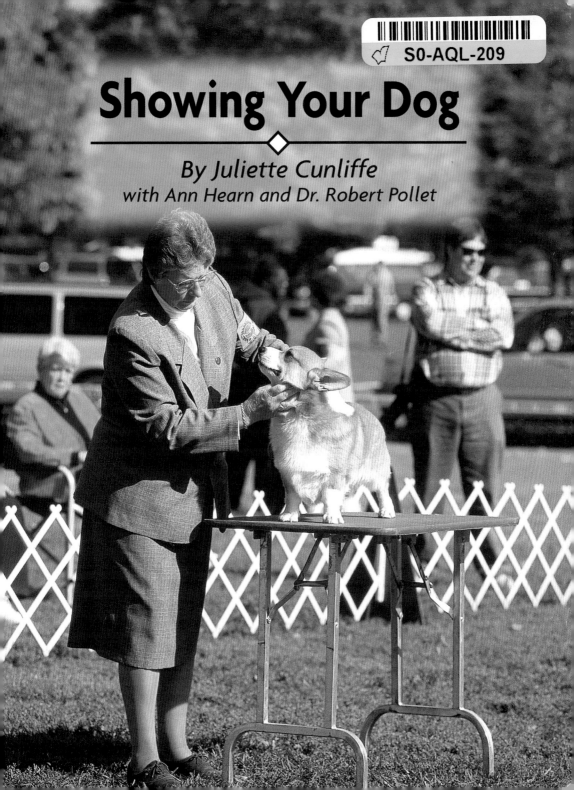

Showing Your Dog

◇

By Juliette Cunliffe

with Ann Hearn and Dr. Robert Pollet

Showing Your Dog

A KENNEL CLUB BOOK™

Photographs by Mary Bloom,
Booth Photography, Juliette Cunliffe,
David Dalton, Karl Donvil, Cheryl Ertelt, Isabelle
Francais, Carol Ann Johnson,
Alice Roche, Nikki Sussman and Alice van Kempen.

KENNEL CLUB BOOKS: **SHOWING YOUR DOG**
ISBN: 1-59378-398-1

Copyright © 2004
Kennel Club Books, Inc., 308 Main Street, Allenhurst, NJ 07711 USA
Cover Design Patented: US 6,435,559 B2 • Printed in South Korea

Contents

Many breed clubs stage their own shows, for their breed only. These specialty shows are wonderful meeting places for people in the breed, as well as good venues for fanciers to observe their chosen breed in action, meet breeders and handlers and gain valuable information.

INTRODUCTION

SO, YOU WANT TO SHOW?

Those of us who genuinely love dogs invariably do so for many reasons. Dogs give us enormous pleasure, unending loyalty and rewarding companionship and, through them, we usually meet numerous like-minded people so that our circle of friends grows.

One of the many ways in which we can enjoy our dogs is by participating in dog shows. Some shows are simply for fun; in others, exhibitors pay high entry fees for the chance to compete for championship titles and other accolades. In most countries, there is a range of other types of shows in between. Some of these are just for one breed, some are for a group of certain breeds (such as all sizes of Poodles, Dachshunds of different sizes and coat types, pointing breeds, etc.) and some are all-breed shows.

Single-breed shows provide wonderful opportunities for relatively new exhibitors to learn more about their chosen breed. Competition is strong, but the atmosphere is usually quite casual, with the emphasis not only on the competitive side of dogdom but also on enjoyment and meeting other breed enthusiasts. Usually there are social events, raffles to raise funds for the club or for some other good cause for the breed, demonstrations and other fun things to do along with the show. Between the classes in which they are exhibiting their dogs, breeders and exhibitors find time to chat and to catch up with each other, and, most importantly, to discuss their breed.

Newcomers to a breed have an opportunity to watch many dogs being judged and to form their own opinions as to which breeding lines they prefer. This will help them to gain an "eye for a dog" and will put them in good stead when they progress to establishing their own breeding lines if this is their pursuit. They will also have opportunities to speak to many experienced breeders and exhibitors, many of whom will also be judges. The newcomer will be able to learn a great deal, though he must always be aware that not everyone to whom he speaks is as knowledgeable as they might appear. Sadly, not everyone has the breed's best interests at heart. As the newcomer becomes more and more involved in the show scene, he will soon find out which breeders he respects and which he would prefer to give a wide berth.

It is only human nature that dog owners treat their dogs in different ways, largely dependent on their personal circumstances and environments. But from the very outset, it is important to realize that a dog is very much more than "just" a show dog. For many of us, showing is a very large part of our involvement with dogs, but not all dogs selected for their show potential will meet their owners' high expectations. This does not mean that the owners will have to part with their much-loved companions, for there are many other activities in which they can participate.

Owners may decide just to have some fun by attending shows at a lower level of competition, or they may choose a different area of the dog sport by entering competitive obedience training or agility work. They may be able to join a flyball team. There is even a competitive sport known as freestyle or heelwork to music, in which dog and handler perform a "dance" routine; this is great fun for the agile among us and certainly entertaining for all to watch. Another avenue that might be of interest, if a dog has a

wonderfully sound temperament, is some sort of therapy work. This might involve visiting senior citizens' homes and hospices so that those less fortunate healthwise can share in a dog's companionship even though they are not able to keep pets of their own. All of these activities reap their own just rewards.

For many, it is the social side of dog showing that attracts them, with winning awards being just the icing on the cake. Many dog-show enthusiasts have their own motor homes that they drive from show to show, taking them all around the country, sometimes actually spending little time in their permanent homes during the height of the show season, which in most countries is during the summer months. Although I am not involved personally in this side of the show scene, I know that there is quite a community of these travelers, who all seem to get along well with each other. Sometimes they even arrange their own events during the evenings after showing has ended.

There are other people who enjoy the organizational aspects of shows. Some of these people show dogs themselves and therefore combine the two. Others, often past owners of dogs, enjoy stewarding in the ring and, over the years, become quite famous show personalities in their own right.

When you have had a certain amount of experience as an exhibitor and perhaps as a breeder, there are usually opportunities to become involved in committee work for a breed club or all-breed canine society. Committee work is usually renowned for being fraught with stress, but it is always good to put something back into the world of dogs, which has given you so much pleasure. Added to this, working on a committee can be a great deal of fun and, although sometimes time-consuming, can be another way of enlarging your circle of friends.

When you become really involved with your chosen breed, you will of course want to attend breed seminars, for they provide ideal opportunities to learn more. Frequently at these seminars, there is an opportunity to do "hands-on" examination of dogs, thus enabling you to assess structure and breed type. Such seminars are usually

Dog shows introduce the dog-loving public to old favorites as well as interesting new faces. The Spinone Italiano is a relative newcomer to AKC showing, while European fanciers have long been acquainted with this Italian charmer.

hosted by breed clubs, or sometimes by general canine societies, and speakers are usually invited because of their knowledge of the featured breed.

So it quickly becomes apparent that there is so much more to showing your dog than immediately meets the eye. I hope that this book will help you to understand how to get the most out of showing your dog, on whatever continent you live and in whatever country.

Always keep first and foremost in your mind that ownership of a dog is not simply ownership of a commodity. A dog is much, much more than that, and you and your dog will hopefully spend many happy years of enjoyment together, both in and out of the show ring.

STEWARDING

Stewarding is something to be learned, as it involves a good knowledge of ring procedure. In some countries, novice judges have to do a certain amount of stewarding before they can progress with their judging careers. Depending on the country, stewards are rewarded in different ways, sometimes just by way of a free lunch, but this is ideal for someone who likes to enjoy a day among dog folk.

ABOVE: At early shows, dog showing was largely a "gentleman's sport" and female exhibitors were very much in the minority. BELOW: But how times change! Here is a scene from the Skye Terrier judging at a Ladies' Kennel Association show around 1900.

HISTORICAL PERSPECTIVE

Events that can loosely be described as dog shows have been taking place for thousands of years, and certainly by the 18th century there were shows that would seem at least remotely familiar to exhibitors today. Hound shows, the first of which took place in Britain in 1776, were organized to help fellow hunstmen keep in contact with each other outside the hunting season, during the summer months.

The agricultural shows of the late 18th century included categories for dogs, and by then the value of dogs as companions had also become greatly appreciated by townsfolk. There was an increasing change in attitude

toward some of the more brutal sports involving dogs, and by the end of the century a growing sentiment of humane treatment had led to protests against bullbaiting, in which dogs had, of course, been involved. However, it was not until 1835 that bullbaiting, cockfighting and dogfighting were officially abolished in Britain.

Shows thrived in both urban and rural localities during the early part of the 19th century, but it was not until the advent of railway travel that those involved in "the fancy" were able to travel to participate in the sport of which they were becoming increasingly fond. That which has become widely known as "the very first dog show" was held in the New

The classes for dogs at agricultural shows preceded formal conformation showing as we know it. These early shows were a bit more chaotic, as we can see in this scene from an agricultural show circa 1863.

THE FANCY EVOLVES

The mid-19th century was a time during which more delicate canine sports were coming into fashion. In 1834, a show was held for "9-lb spaniels," and the prize was a silver cream jug. This event took place in the undoubtedly less delicate venue of a public drinking house; it was in such establishments that the actual sport of dog showing began.

Corn Exchange at Newcastle-on-Tyne in the north of England on June 28 and 29, 1859. Thanks to the advent of the train, exhibitors came from far away; at least one of the judges traveled all the way from London.

This dog show was held as part of a well-established poultry show, and breed competition was restricted to Pointers and Setters, although other dogs and puppies were at the show for exhibition only, rather than for competition. The show was highly praised for its organization, with the dogs being chained and protected by barriers so that they could neither injure nor alarm visitors to the show. There were 23 Pointers entered, and the best one was awarded one of Pape's celebrated double-barreled guns, worth between £15 and £20. There were 36 entries in the Setter class, the winner of which also received a double-barreled gun.

At this important show, one of the judges was Mr. J. H. Walsh, then editor of *The Field* and now best known for his literary works under the guise of "Stonehenge." He became one of the organizers of the next show, which took place later that year in Birmingham, a real stronghold of England's dog fancy.

As the 19th century progressed, the popularity of dog shows increased. In 1862, a show at the New Agricultural Hall in London's Islington brought in an entry of 803, and in May 1863 another show in London, called "The First International Dog Show," mustered an entry of 1,678. However, many of the entries actually comprised several dogs, so it was believed that there were probably over 2,000 dogs in the hall.

Dog showing goes global! Many international fanciers visited England for the 1934 Kennel Club Show held at the Crystal Palace in London.

In March of the same year, "The First Annual Grand National Exhibition of Sporting and Other Dogs" was held in Chelsea, England. This show attracted great publicity and, from it, many lessons were learned. The organizers' laborers were said to have been overwhelmed by the difficulties of the endeavor. Although there was an ornamental fountain in the middle of the building, there was no provision of water for the dogs, which were crowded together with no divisions between them. The building had a glass roof, so it was always either too hot or too cold inside. Instead of being issued numbers, each exhibit had a label attached to his collar, giving the name and address of the dog's owner. This meant that the judges knew exactly which dog belonged to whom, something that could indeed have had some bearing on their final awards.

To find any particular dog was an unenviable task, for often, when

the specified location was reached, the dog was either absent from the show completely, not where he should be or did not correspond with his description. A prime example was that of "Wolf, brought from Crimea," on whose bench was a litter of puppies. Future organizers certainly took heed, and in the coming years became much more careful in making suitable arrangements for their shows.

In the mid-19th century the majority of dog fanciers were not part of society's elite. With the intervention of England's Kennel Club, though, in the latter part of the 19th century, a certain

Dog showing caught on with royalty, both as exhibitors and spectators, like visitors King Edward VII and Queen Alexandra.

ROYAL FAVORITES

With royalty's active role in dog showing, it is evident that, at times, these noble exhibitors were granted special treatment. For example, when Queen Victoria wished to exhibit three of her Pomeranians of a color not usually shown, a special class was provided for her dogs. Two of them were lucky enough to be awarded joint first prize!

respectability was brought to dog showing and many eminent persons began to participate. Queen Victoria was an exhibitor and, in 1875, the Prince of Wales became Patron of The Kennel Club, continuing his patronage following his accession to the throne as King Edward VII. He was an active breeder and occasional exhibitor of several breeds; Queen Alexandra was identified mainly with Borzois, Basset Hounds, Chow Chows, Skye Terriers, Japanese Spaniels and Pugs. The royal couple regularly visited shows and took pleasure in going along the benches, often stopping to talk to the dogs along their way. King George V was mainly involved with Labradors and Clumber Spaniels; although he showed occasionally, his primary concern was that his dogs could do a good day's work.

The nobility played a very active part in dog showing, especially Her Grace the Duchess of Newcastle, who did much to raise the tone of shows by her personal patronage. The Countess of Aberdeen was also very prominent, with her deep love of Skye Terriers, inherited from her father, Lord Tweedmouth. At shows then, just as today, dogs brought together people from all walks of life, though certain exhibitors were undoubtedly favored.

In the early years, dog-showing enthusiasts were primarily men, but the subsequent involvement of high-ranking ladies brought a certain air of elegance to the sport. This opened up doors for others of the fairer sex, and today dog showing is enjoyed by all, whatever their upbringing, sex or indeed sexual persuasion.

The annual Crufts Dog Show is the most important canine event in the UK, just as Westminster is in the US and the World Dog Show is in Europe. This photograph of the 1934 Crufts show, held at the Royal Agricultural Hall, London, depicts judging in full swing.

Sealyham Terrier judging at a Terrier Championship Show in 1932.

Circa 1930, Bull Terriers and Airedale Terriers in their respective rings, awaiting judging at a Joint-Terrier show.

SELECTING YOUR BREED

If the idea of showing dogs has attracted you, you will have to make an important decision about exactly which breed you would like to show. Unless you are extremely lucky, your family pet, although much loved and enormously attractive in your eyes, is not likely to be of suitably high quality for exhibition at shows, other than small shows that are really just for fun. There can be exceptions, but it's a one-in-a-million chance.

So let's assume that you are in a position to actually select the breed you would most like to take into the ring. Of course, you will be guided by your personal preferences. It may be that you decide to stay with the same breed as your family pet. This time, when picking your potential show dog, you will have to be extra-discerning about both the puppy you choose and the breeder from whom you decide to buy.

At this stage, you are keeping an open mind. There are many basic factors to consider, so let's discuss them here in more detail.

SIZE

The size of the breed you choose may not be purely a matter of your personal likes and dislikes. There are many people who love large breeds but find themselves unable to manage a large dog's weight, height and strength. Thus, not only would they be unable to cope with such a dog around the home but they also could not do the dog (and themselves) justice in the show ring.

Granted, at a dog show you will see many frail-looking or elderly people with giant breeds that seem fully under control, but you must bear in mind that such people have probably had this breed for decades and know exactly how to manage it. If you are already well past middle age, taking on for the first time a large, heavy breed with a strong character is unlikely to be a wise move. Of course, large breeds can be remarkably obedient, but a new owner must know exactly how to treat the dog so that he is completely manageable.

Your physical strength must be taken into account, and you should also keep in mind that a

FACING PAGE: Oftentimes families are in a breed for many generations and you will see experienced handlers at shows who themselves have had the same breed for decades. The Deerhound has many multi-generation handlers in its fancy.

small, sturdy, low-set breed, such as the Bulldog or Staffordshire Bull Terrier, has great strength and thus can be just as physically demanding as one of the tall, long-legged breeds. Should your choice be a German Shepherd Dog, or perhaps a long-legged dog such as an Afghan Hound, you will need sufficient stamina to gait the dog at the correct speed, as many times as the judge desires, if you are to show the dog to his best advantage.

On the other hand, if you are at all clumsy or slow in your reaction time, or if your sight is impaired, one of the tiny toy breeds may not be a wise choice, for they can all too easily be stumbled over. As many of them move very quickly, they can be under your feet before you know it.

Thankfully, there is a wide range of breeds that fall in between the very large and the very small, and you are certain to find one that you like and that suits you, whatever your personal preferences and physical capabilities.

COAT

Apart from your personal preferences as to the esthetic appeal of a particular coat type, a very important consideration will be how much time you are prepared to put into coat care. Even the shortest coated breed will need some care, but this will be minimal compared

WORKS OF ART

The Poodle and certain terrier breeds, like the Bedlington, are fine examples of breeds that are actually sculpted into shape, and this is indeed an art that needs to be learned. Some breeds also have topknots, and it is surprising how much difference the correct set of a topknot can make in a dog's expression, enhancing or ruining his chance of winning high honors.

Some breeds require much grooming, including elaborate preparations right before the show. The Old English Sheepdog is one such example, requiring intense pre-show work on the part of the groomer.

Showing requires much travel, so breed portability will factor into your decision. Do you have a suitably-sized vehicle to accommodate a larger breed and everything you need to take along to the show?

with longer-coated dogs. Many of the terriers and other wire-coated breeds need their coats to be stripped, largely by hand, involving many hours of dedicated work and skill. Consider, too, that even if a breed's coat is not especially long, such as that of the Bearded Collie or Shetland Sheepdog, some of the breeds with medium-length coats also involve a great deal of work.

Yet another factor to consider is whether or not anyone in your family is allergic to dogs. If this is the case, this factor will weigh heavily on your decision as to which breed you choose. The coats of some breeds seem to affect some allergy sufferers and yet not others, so you will have to give much thought to the subject and allow the person concerned to spend time in the company of the breed you like before coming to a final decision.

NUMERICAL STRENGTH

Showing can be great fun, but the general idea of showing is to win or at least to gain a place in your class. Thus you may wish to consider the numerical strength of the breed you choose. In some breeds, such as Labrador and Golden Retrievers, Border Collies and Rottweilers, there can be hundreds of dogs entered at a show, making for very large entries in each class. On the other hand, many breeds have only a few entries at each show, so the chances of winning are substantially increased, even though a dog still has to get past some high-quality exhibits if they are present on that day.

CHAMPIONSHIP STATUS

Another factor to consider, especially if you decide on one of the lesser-known breeds, is whether or not that breed already has championship status in the country or countries in which you will be exhibiting. In some countries, winning the title of Champion is a great honor, though those of us who are steeped in the dog-showing scene realize that in other countries, winning the title of

UPS AND DOWNS

Breed numbers, of course, vary very much from country to country, and breeds that are popular in one country may be not so popular in another.

This Junior Handler is proud of her Briards. Junior Handling is open to young handlers, who can enter with any pure-bred breed. The judging is based on the handlers' presentation rather than the dogs themselves.

Champion is not always as significant as the title suggests.

Exhibiting one of the rare breeds, or breeds not yet fully recognized by the national kennel club(s), will mean that the title of Champion in some countries simply will not be available to that breed because it has been neither bred nor shown in significant numbers to warrant championship status. Once again, though, this does vary from country to country.

GENERAL CONSIDERATIONS

Keeping a show dog in tip-top condition takes time, patience and money, aside from the actual cost

of entering a show, transportation and meals away from home. You may even have to purchase a different vehicle to comfortably accommodate the breed of your choice and his accessories.

If you have a long-coated breed, there will be a substantial initial outlay involved in the cost of grooming equipment, which, apart from a grooming table, brushes, combs, scissors, tweezers, shampoos and conditioners, may involve a special canine hair-dryer, which can amount to a hefty sum. Your grooming table must be of a type that's easy to take along to shows, and of course you will need a dog crate. Perhaps you can find a clever contraption that doubles as both.

At home, unless you have one of the small breeds, you may decide that you need a special exercise area in your yard so that your dog has a specific place in which to run and to rest. Thus you may also need a kennel or suitable dog run for this purpose. The type of setup you will need, of course, depends very much on the breed, but in any event you will have to be absolutely certain that your home and yard are entirely dog-proof.

All things considered, you will realize that, even though you may be certain that you want to show your dog, the actual selection of your breed will be a very important factor from the outset.

FOOD FACTOR

When selecting your breed, you may also wish to take into account the cost of feeding, bearing in mind that a giant-breed dog will eat substantially more than a tiny one.

SELECTING YOUR BREEDER

DOING YOUR RESEARCH

Now that you have selected the breed that you wish to show, you will have to locate a good breeder with puppies available for sale. Indeed, to get what you want from a breeder of repute, you may have to wait, especially in the rarer breeds in which litters are produced only occasionally.

You should by now have visited a few shows. At these shows, you will have gained some idea of which breeders seem to be producing stock that pleases your eye. Observe the temperaments of the dogs bred by these people, and you should also take a more-than-cursory glance at the temperaments of the breeders themselves. What you need is a breeder who shows that he genuinely cares for his dogs, treating them with kindness both inside the show ring and out. A genuinely devoted breeder raises all of his puppies with love, care and attention. This is highly important, for a puppy that has received little or no human affection in the early weeks of life is likely to find it difficult to adjust to new situations as he matures.

You may wish to consider whether you want to buy from a major breeder, who probably has a large kennel of dogs, or from someone who breeds fewer litters, primarily as a hobby. There are pros and cons to each. The breeder who produces only one or two litters a year is likely to spend more time with the puppies than someone who breeds one or more litters a month. Having said that, the latter probably has devoted kennel helpers who assist in giving the youngsters necessary social contact.

Although not always the case, the smaller breeder is more likely to raise the puppies in his home, which means that the pups are exposed to things like hearing the clatter of saucepans and the noise of the vacuum cleaner. Having had these experiences and other exposure to everyday life, the puppies will probably find it easier to adapt to their new home environments when they leave with new owners.

Of course, those breeders who breed fewer litters are less likely to have puppies of show potential available for sale, as many of them will keep the picks of the litters for

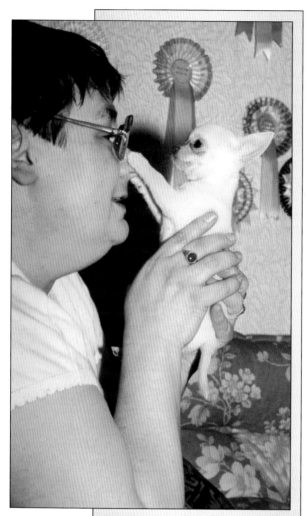

SHOW POTENTIAL

Keep in mind that no breeder, however good, can sell a puppy as a "show puppy." Although breeders can have a good idea how their stock will mature, all sorts of things can go wrong as the youngsters grow to maturity, so an honest breeder will merely say that a puppy has "show potential."

themselves. On the other hand, if the breeder's pick is a bitch when your own preference is for a male, you may be able to obtain the pick of the males. The eventual decision has to be your own, but of ultimate importance is that you buy from someone you can trust, even if it means you have to wait a while or travel a long distance.

There are two other important factors to consider when you are visiting a show in these early stages. First, if a breeder only takes into the ring dogs that have been bred by others, it may mean that home-bred dogs from that kennel are not yet up to par. Second, it is also worth keeping an eye out to see which breeders have sold good stock that is winning well in the hands of others.

If this is your first show dog and you have bought from a good breeder, this breeder will be of infinite help to you in the weeks and months ahead. Apart from hints about nutrition, exercise and grooming equipment, the breeder will be able to tell you if you are presenting the dog correctly in the ring, if you are moving the dog too quickly or too slowly or if perhaps you are entering a class that is too great a challenge. An experienced breeder who also exhibits with success will be able to advise you as to which judges are likely to appreciate his or her stock.

If your visits to dog shows and the inquiries and contacts made at the shows have not led you to a suitable breeder with stock for sale in the near future, you may wish to pursue other avenues in your search. A useful source of information about potential litters is your country's canine press. Remember, though, just because a breeder advertises in this manner, it does not necessarily mean that he or she is a good breeder, so you will still have to exercise care.

Most countries have national breed clubs as well as regional and local clubs that may be affiliated with the national club. The secretaries of these clubs are usually very helpful in pointing you toward member breeders in your region, and they may even know which breeders have stock available for sale. To find such clubs for your chosen breed, contact the national kennel club with whom you wish to register and show your dog. A quick telephone call or e-mail should give you the information you need. Of course, it will be very convenient if a good breeder lives locally and happens to have just the puppy you want, but, again, you should be prepared to travel to visit some breeders and see their litters.

VISITING LITTERS

Before arranging a visit to a kennel, it is only fair to the breeder to make it perfectly clear that you are looking for a puppy that will hopefully be of sufficient

GENTLE JUDGES

An interesting tip that your breeder should be able to share is which judges are known to be gentle with dogs and which have a tendency to be more heavy-handed. You may wish to avoid the latter, at least during puppyhood. Likewise, owners of small-breed dogs would be wise to know which judges are more careful in their handling.

quality to show. You should also state if you have a preference for a dog or a bitch. Know what you want before you visit. Breeders are often very busy people and do not take kindly to those who waste their time by visiting when they have absolutely no intention of even considering a puppy from the available litter.

When going to visit a litter, the breeder should always give you the opportunity to see the dam as well as the pups. Observe how she interacts with her offspring, for often the puppies' temperaments will be similar to hers. Although she should look clean and tidy, you must take into account when assessing her appearance that she has been raising a litter of little ones, which will almost undoubtedly have

taken their toll. Do not necessarily expect to see the sire, for it is likely that he is owned by someone else and therefore not on the premises. You should, however, be given the chance to see a photograph of the sire and to have the puppies' pedigree explained.

It is of the utmost importance that, if you have selected a breed that is prone to certain health problems, the breeder shows you documentation certifying that the pups have been deemed healthy by a vet and that the breeding stock tested clear of hereditary problems and is suitable to be bred from. Hereditary problems can be seen in most breeds, and reputable breeders only breed from stock that has been tested and that has proven to be free of any such problems.

Sometimes breeders bring their puppies to shows. It's fun for people to meet them and it provides important socialization for the litter.

This lovely lady and her winning Italian Greyhound, Artemis Robins Rachel, are typical of the people and dogs on their way to championships. It takes skill, perseverance and a winning attitude.

WHAT TO LOOK FOR IN A SHOW PUPPY

Part of the reason for carefully selecting the breeder from whom you want to buy is that, if this is your first show dog, you will be largely reliant on his opinion as to which puppy will be most suitable to take into the show ring. All of the puppies in a litter will inevitably look sweet, but it is highly unlikely that all of them will have equal show potential.

Depending on the breed you have chosen, there will be a variety of factors to take into consideration such as breed type, soundness of construction and, not least, personality. In some breeds there are obvious signs, such as the amount of white on the body. In some breeds, for example, the allowable amount of white is specified in the breed standard. In these cases, it will be perfectly evident that a dog with white up to his elbows, when the breed is only allowed white on its toes, will simply not be the one to choose.

Other things are less strikingly obvious, and in some cases only the breeder will know how the puppy is likely to develop. In some breeds, especially those with a reverse scissor or undershot bite in adulthood, the jaw placement will alter as the puppy grows and develops. This means that a puppy with a scissor bite at ten weeks old may well have the desired reverse scissor bite by six months of age. If the bite is already "correct" as a baby, chances are it will be too undershot by the time the pup is old enough for the show ring. This is just one of many examples I could choose, but the list is endless. If you do not yet have sufficient experience, you will have to rely heavily on the breeder's recommendations and advice. Bear in mind that the breeder will not want inferior stock to represent his kennel in the ring, so it also is to the breeder's benefit to guide you correctly.

If you read the standard for your chosen breed before going to visit the puppies, this will put you in very good stead and you will have an idea of the desirable (and undesirable) points to look for. If, for example, a black nose is required in your breed, but the nose of the puppy you like is not completely black, you will be able to ask the breeder whether or not the nose is likely to correct itself with maturity. Again this will vary from breed to breed, as well as from line to line within a breed. However, if you have studied your standard and have looked at photographs of high-quality and champion dogs in a canine annual or magazine, you will be much better equipped when you visit to view the litter.

It goes without saying that the puppy you buy should be in good health. All puppies in the litter should be clean and free from parasites, with no signs of discharge from their eyes or noses, and there should be no evidence of loose stools.

PUPPY PERSONALITY

Although all breeds are different, puppies that are destined to be in the show ring need to have plenty of confidence, so don't be tempted to select the pretty sweet thing that hides under the table just because you have taken pity on the pup. The puppy you select should have that "look at me" atti-

A young Bouvier endures his pre-show grooming with a friendly "smile." This is the type of disposition you want in a show dog.

tude and a happy personality. Although he should be confident, he should not show signs of being overly dominant with his siblings or you may have trouble on your hands if you have, or plan to have, other dogs in your home. That said, I cannot stress sufficiently that a great deal depends upon the breed you have chosen.

GAUGING GROWTH

Growth patterns vary within certain lines in each breed. This, again, is where a dedicated breeder can be invaluable, for he will know how his particular line is likely to develop, taking into account, of course, the stud dog that has been used.

A DOG OR A BITCH?

You may have a personal preference for the sex of your potential show dog. If you do, don't allow the breeder to sway you into taking a puppy of the opposite sex against your better judgment.

However, because you plan to show your puppy, this may have some bearing on the sex you

PEDIGREE VS. REGISTRATION CERTIFICATE

New owners are very often confused about the differences between a pup's pedigree and registration. The pedigree is essentially a family tree, a written record of a dog's genealogy of three generations or more that lists the names as well as performance titles of all the dogs in your pup's background. Your breeder must provide you with a registration application, with his part properly filled out. You must complete the application and send it to the registering kennel club with the proper fee. In order to be registered, the puppy must be pure-bred and of a breed recognized by that organization, and must meet any other requirements set forth by the registering body.

The seller must provide you with complete records to identify the puppy. This information includes breed; sex, color and markings; date of birth; litter number (when available); names and registration numbers of the parents; breeder's name; and date sold or delivered.

choose. It is generally frowned upon to a take a bitch to a show when she is in season, so there may well be shows that you would like to take her to, but cannot. Although some exhibitors use veterinary services to delay a bitch's season at the height of her show campaign, I would certainly never recommend this, as it can play havoc with her breeding cycle and sometimes her temperament as well. If you have a bitch, you will also find that many lose coat following a season, so this will be a time when she won't be looking her best for the ring.

In many breeds, males are more striking to look at because they carry more coat. This is especially so in those breeds that carry a ruff around the neck. However, it is often difficult to keep males together at home, though this will vary according to the breed, and even according to different lines within a breed. Do not run into the trap of overloading yourself with too many males during your first flush of enthusiasm as an exhibitor; this is an easy thing to do, as often breeders are happier to part with good dogs than good bitches. The latter they have a tendency to keep for themselves!

AGE AT WHICH TO BUY

In some countries, the kennel club or breed club specifies the minimum age at which a puppy should be sold. In any case, it is usually sensible not to purchase a puppy destined for the show ring when he is too young. Different breeds mature at different rates, so your breeder can help you project your dog's development. In some breeds, to be as sure as possible that the puppy will go on to be as good as anticipated, it is wise not to buy until around 16 weeks or even later. This is often the case in a breed where the teeth and jaws take more time to develop. Other breeds are better off if they move to their new homes earlier, either because the breed's personality demands this in order to settle easily into a new environment or because "what you see at eight weeks is (pretty much) what you get." It has to be said that, in some breeds, little is likely to change so dramatically that it would detract from a puppy's show potential, whereas in others much more can go wrong.

"RUNNING ON" A PUPPY

Some breeders are willing to "run on" a puppy until it is about five or six months old. What this means is that the breeder retains the puppy (sometimes two) until it is a little more mature, to better assess whether or not it will be up to the standards for the show ring. In the case of running on more than one puppy, the breeder assesses which of them will be the best prospect. In this case, you will book the puppy in advance and will have to pay a much higher price than if you had bought a pup of eight or ten weeks of age.

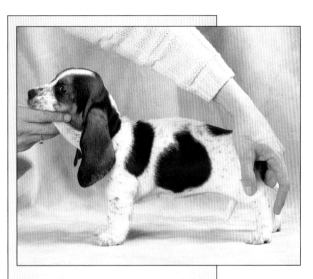

SHOW-QUALITY SHOWS

Although the breeder can guide you, using his experience and knowledge, to the best prospect in the litter if you wish to show, it is impossible to tell, at eight to ten weeks of age, whether your dog will be a contender. Some promising pups end up with minor to serious faults that prevent them from taking home a Best of Breed award, but this certainly does not mean they can't be the best of family companions. To assess your potential show dog's quality, enter him in a match or similar fun-type show to see how a judge evaluates him. Your breeder also can offer advice as the puppy matures.

Something to watch out for when buying a puppy of run-on age, if not booked well in advance, is that the breeder has run the puppy on with the intention of showing, but it has not turned out sufficiently well, hence the decision has been made to sell the pup. Usually the breeder makes a decision between four

It will be helpful if your future star politely tolerates his grooming. This young Sheltie is already learning the ropes of the pre-show routine.

NOVICE PICKS

Unfortunately, it is not easy for a newcomer to buy a really top-quality animal, because most breeders like to keep the very best for themselves. A lot, though, depends on the success of the breeder. The second pick from a good litter bred by an experienced person is often infinitely better than the pick of the litter from a novice breeder who is still learning the ropes.

and six months of age, depending on the breed, though there is no hard-and-fast rule concerning this.

BUYING AN OLDER PUPPY OR ADULT DOG

Another possibility for a new exhibitor is to buy a dog that has already been in the show ring. Sometimes a breeder may campaign a youngster for a few shows with the intention of selling the pup at a high price when he already has some success under his belt (or collar!). Just occasionally, an older dog of good quality may be for sale because a breeder has more stock than he can campaign successfully, or even because of conflict of temperament between the dogs at home. However, if an older dog is of really high quality, the price will be commensurate, and the breeder may not be willing to let the dog go to anyone other than an exhibitor who has a proven record of success in the ring.

PREPARING YOUR PUPPY FOR THE SHOW RING

If you are lucky, your puppy will have received a little training from his breeder, especially if you have made it clear that you want to show. For many puppies destined for show homes, breeders begin gentle training, such as standing on a table, from the age of around six weeks. However, once you have collected your puppy, training becomes entirely your responsibility. Always remember that a well-trained puppy stands a much greater chance of success at shows.

Trained or not, when your puppy moves to his new home, your home, he will probably be thrown into confusion. In the first few days, training should be kept to a bare minimum, giving the youngster time to settle in. Introductions should be made to all who live in the home, giving the puppy the chance to get used to people, but please take care that nobody handles him roughly. Other pets in the household should also be introduced, but exercise caution as to the way they might react to one another.

PRE-INOCULATION

Depending on the age of your puppy, his inoculation program may or may not be complete. Vaccines vary, and you must take the vet's advice as to when your puppy can meet other dogs with full protection from disease. Don't be over-enthusiastic about socializing your puppy away from your home territory before the time is right. If the pup's vaccinations are not complete and you have to take him to the vet for his final shots, please carry the pup, rather than walk him, into the vet's clinic. If he is already too big for that, ask the vet to come out to your car.

THE EARLY WEEKS OF TRAINING

Training does not just involve practicing with your pup for performance in the ring. Teaching

INSURANCE

Something to consider is whether or not to take out veterinary insurance for your dog. You may find that the first few weeks have been covered by the breeder, which gives you time to consider the best options. As veterinary insurance is becoming more popular with owners, the range of coverage is growing.

your puppy to enjoy grooming sessions is also very important, particularly if yours is a coated breed. Most dogs, if trained sensibly from an early age, will readily accept being taught to lie over on their sides. This is, of course, especially helpful for long-coated breeds, but it can make checking between the foot-pads, clipping toenails and inspecting ears considerably easier for dogs of any breed. Such training can also pay dividends when visiting the vet or when you need to apply eye or ear treatment.

Teaching a dog to lie on his side takes practice. To get started, you should stand your dog on a table (unless he is too large, in which case you will work on the floor). Grasp the upper part of the dog's legs on the side that is farther away from you and, leaning over him with your body, gently ease him down on his side. As soon as your dog gets to know what is expected of him, he will virtually roll over of his own

accord, provided he has learned to associate the process with something pleasurable, such as a tummy rub.

The first few times you do this, just give your puppy attention and fuss when he is in the proper position. Then slowly start to introduce a soft brush. Never cause him any pain at this early stage for, if you do, you may turn him off to grooming for the rest of his life! Just go through the motions of looking inside his ears and inspecting his toes so that he gets used to your fiddling about with them. Later it will come as no surprise when you clip his nails or pluck his ears gently with the tweezers.

Many dogs are reluctant to lie down when being dried with a blow dryer, so you also should begin accustoming your pup to this at the beginning of your grooming training. During your practice sessions, switch on the dryer in the background to let the puppy get used to the noise. When you eventually start the drying process, be careful not to pull at any knots or otherwise hurt him, or he will associate the dryer with pain. Also take care that the airflow is neither too hot nor too cold. Clearly some dogs take more easily to grooming sessions than others, but if you have a well-trained dog, you will find that grooming is thoroughly pleasurable for both of you.

FIRM BUT FAIR

By all means be firm, but never yell at or hit the puppy for misbehaving; that will only serve to do considerably more harm than good. You should be aiming to build up his respect for you, so that he looks upon you as "top dog." To earn his respect, you must be kind and fair.

TEACHING YOUR PUPPY TO STAND

A very important aspect of training for the show ring is getting your puppy used to standing still when required. In the show ring, a medium-sized or large-breed dog will have to stand on the floor only, but judges usually examine smaller breeds on a table and sometimes on the ground as well. In this case, you will need to get your puppy used to standing on both surfaces. Make sure that the table you use to practice standing has a non-slip surface, for if the pup does not feel sure of his footing, or if the table wobbles, this will cause difficulties.

Practice standing your puppy with his head facing your right, for this is the most usual direction in which he will be shown. In some countries, though not all, it is permissible to stand a dog in the opposite direction, something that is frequently done if a dog has more esthetically appealing markings on one side, for example. There are other exceptions, such as with the Pekingese and the Bulldog, which are usually shown head-on.

In most breeds, your aim will be to teach your dog to stand with his feet placed naturally below his body, so that his weight is evenly placed on all four feet. A notable exception is the German Shepherd Dog, which calls for one of the hind legs to be extended backwards slightly. If you have visited a few shows to study your breed before entering your puppy at shows, you will soon get to know what is expected.

"Stand" is the usual command, using a firm voice, with "No" each time the enthusiastic youngster tries to disappear to do something more exciting. You should be able to practice standing almost as soon as you obtain your puppy, once you have given him a couple of days to get used to you and his new home.

A difficult puppy can be reprimanded by staring him in the eyes while holding him firmly by the scruff of his neck. Obviously, you have to make sure that his back end is supported. The reprimand must be given at the very moment he misbehaves, so that he knows exactly what he is doing wrong. Take care, though, that no accident happens, and don't place your face too close to his, for it is surprising

Teaching the dog to stand on a grooming table has dual benefits with a small breed, as the table is used not just for grooming but also in the ring for evaluation by the judge.

The type of collar and lead used in the show ring is different from the type you will use for training and everyday walks.

how quickly a young puppy can dart forward, albeit in play.

When practicing standing, a very useful aid is a mirror, so that you can see exactly how your puppy would look to the judge. Different breeds are shown differently and it is important that, when you and your puppy finally end up in the ring, you present your exhibit to perfection according to the requirements for your particular breed.

COLLAR AND LEAD
Even if your puppy is not yet fully vaccinated and able to go out in public places, you can still carry out training in the confines of your home. The pup will, of course, need to get used to the feel of a collar and lead around his neck. When the collar is initially introduced, it will seem very strange to him, for he will have the feeling of being restricted. The collar must not be too tight, nor should it be too loose for fear of his getting caught up in something and throwing himself into a panic or possibly being injured. Obviously, you will have to keep adjusting the collar to make it larger or buying larger collars as he matures.

When introducing the collar, be sure that there are no other animals around to distract him. Since the pup should have total confidence in you, this is an exercise best done while you are alone. Let him smell the collar first, then, holding him firmly, gently slip it over his head. Sooner or later he will realize that there is something around his neck and will most probably paw at it in an attempt to free himself. He may also try to rub his head along the ground or around the bottom of the sofa or something similar, trying to release his head.

Practice for very short periods at first, always under supervision, never allowing the puppy to work himself up into too much of a frenzy before the collar is taken off. Within a few short days, you will find that he accepts the collar perfectly.

When the puppy is confident wearing his collar, it is time to introduce the lead. This can prove to be infinitely more difficult than introducing the collar, though some puppies take to the lead much more easily than others. Ideally, you should choose a lead that can be attached to the collar with which the puppy is already familiar. It must have a trigger mechanism, rather than the sort that just slips in; the latter type can easily become loose if the puppy pulls in the wrong direction and thus is very dangerous.

Many successful show-goers have their own preferences as to how to introduce a lead, and a great deal will depend upon the tractability of your own puppy. You want him to concentrate on the task at hand, so, once again, ensure that there are no distractions. Use a flat area, free of clutter, preferably without too many interesting aromas. Your puppy must associate his lead with pleasure, so you must be in a happy frame of mind. Always remember that your own positive or negative emotions will travel down the lead to your pup!

If your puppy is bewildered by the whole affair and just stands still, hold the end of the lead and move, in backwards fashion, to the lead's length, so you are in front of the puppy with the length of the lead between you. Then encourage him to come toward you, giving a gentle tug on the lead if necessary. Give him encouragement throughout the process, and you may want to reward him with a little tidbit when he has reached you successfully. Always give him lots of praise when he comes to you. Never practice for too long at a time, but for several short sessions each day.

BUILDING CONFIDENCE

It is essential that all early training be carried out in a perfectly safe environment, taking care that nothing will occur that might cause a setback. When the puppy is confident on his collar and lead in his own environment, it will be time to take him out into the big wide world, where he will encounter sights and smells that he has never before experienced. He will soon get over the initial shock, but remember that he must always have implicit faith in you, so be sure that you instill confidence in him at all times. Eventually, it will be a good experience to walk your youngster in noisy places, but build up to this gradually so that he never has to cope with too much too soon.

PRACTICE AT HOME

You and your future champion can prepare for the ring by holding mock trials at home in your yard, with family and friends as the audience. You must train him to stay in a standing position, to gait by your side at the correct pace and in the proper pattern and to tolerate being handled and examined by the judge. Most breeds require complete dentition, all breeds require a particular bite (scissor, level or undershot) and all males must have two apparently normal testicles fully descended into the scrotum. The dog must behave politely during a full evaluation.

Should yours be a puppy that prefers to scamper about when the lead is attached, he is unlikely to respond readily to the aforementioned method. Because he is clearly not at the stage when you can actually lead him anywhere, let him take you. Follow him wherever he wants to go (within reason), all the while holding the end of the lead firmly, but not restraining him in any way initially. If he suddenly realizes that you are at the end of the lead and puts the brakes on, you can try to gain his confidence by encouraging him to come toward you using the previously described method. "Little and often" is again the motto, and in two or three days you should find that you are able to lead him about.

Once you have some control over the puppy on lead, you can begin to teach him to walk politely with you. Give a gentle tug on the lead, encouraging the puppy to walk next to you on your left-hand side, for this is the side on which he will usually be gaited in the show ring. Don't expect miracles at first, for he would probably prefer to travel in the opposite direction. Provided you keep his confidence at all times, though, using his name, which he should recognize by now, he will soon progress. Never shout at your puppy, and don't be afraid to use a rather foolish-sounding high-pitched tone if that seems to help. If you can overcome your embarrassment now, you will find it much easier to make your entrance into the show ring later on.

PRESENTATION AND CARE

LEARNING THE ROPES

For novice exhibitors, a show handling class to prepare you for the ring can be an ideal learning place for both dog and handler. Indeed, many well-established exhibitors use such classes to practice with their youngsters, but it is important that the class you select is professionally run by experienced people and suitable for your particular breed. Also, be careful not to confuse a show-training class with an obedience-training class. The former is what you need to help train your dog for the show ring.

I personally think that your first visit to a show handling class should primarily be to watch, rather than to participate. This will give you the opportunity to see exactly what is done in the class, how well it is run and also what types of dog are enrolled. If yours is a tiny toy breed and the room is full of giant breeds, you may be wiser to seek a different class. In this instance, it could be that the people who run the class are more familiar with large breeds than with toys, so you and your small dog will not get as

much out of the class. A good way of finding out about these types of classes, and ones that are suitable for your particular breed, is through your national kennel club (AKC, The Kennel Club, etc.) or one of the breed clubs. Your vet may also be able to make some suggestions.

The classes are usually held on a weekly or bi-weekly basis. In these classes, you will not only be able to put your puppy through his paces in the company of other dogs but there also will be people there to give guidance and instruction as to proper ring procedure and how to show your dog to his best. For example, you can receive pointers on how well or how badly your dog is moving, and how this can be corrected if necessary.

LOOKING HIS BEST

Apart from being sure that your puppy is as well trained as possible for his entrance into the show ring, he must also be presented in good physical form, which includes having his coat in top condition.

The specific coat preparation you need will be relevant to your particular breed, so you must seek

KEEP IT CLEAN!

In some breeds, it is virtually considered taboo to bathe a dog at all, but no judge wants to put his hands on a dirty, smelly dog! Regardless of the breed, the coat must be kept clean, resilient and looking nice.

advice from someone experienced in the breed regarding how to care for your dog's coat. You should also arm yourself with books about the breed, as many give step-by-step grooming instructions, often accompanied by photos and illustrations. You may initially want to visit a library to see which books give the most helpful advice before you decide which ones to buy. At bookstores and large dog shows, the range of books on sale can be enormous, particularly if you have one of the numerically stronger breeds. The breeder of your puppy will probably be able to recommend those which he thinks are best.

Coat care is important not just at a show but beforehand and in between, too. Most of the long-coated breeds need routine care on a daily basis, or at least two or three times weekly. No judge will take kindly to discovering a multitude of knots concealed under a glamorous-looking topcoat. The Yorkshire Terriers you see at shows, in all their glory, have probably spent most of their lives indoors with their coats in paper wraps, which is a time-consuming task even for the most dedicated exhibitor.

The shorter- and smooth-coated breeds also need attention to their coats to keep them in good shape between shows, and nutrition is also important in helping the condition of your dog's skin and coat. If a dog's coat looks a little on the dull side, a drop of oil in his diet has been found to help.

While some breeds are bathed very infrequently, others are bathed before each show, possibly on a weekly basis during the height of the show season. This is another factor that you must consider before selecting your breed.

GENERAL PHYSICAL CONDITION
Different breeds mature at different rates, so you must seek advice from your breeder as to how much or how little exercise you should give your puppy during the early months of his life. For many large and giant breeds, it is considered

wise to restrict exercise in puppies because their bones develop at such a fast rate. It is often suggested that free exercise in a limited area be allowed, but that on-lead walks are something to which you will build up very slowly, gradually increasing in length.

The major stipulation for the smaller breeds is that they should never be allowed to jump on and off furniture; in doing so, they run the risk of forcing out their elbows due to their front legs' taking too much pressure as the dog lands. Stairs should also be treated with caution, and it goes without saying that you must take every precaution that accidents of any kind do not happen.

FEEDING

Without correct feeding, no dog will reach peak condition. Some dogs are prone to putting on too much weight, while others find it difficult to keep weight on, so you will have to help your dog strike that happy balance. Weight is an important factor, especially in the case of Miniature Dachshunds, which have to be weighed immediately prior to judging. Many is the exhibitor who has had to walk his Dachshund around the parking lot in the hope that the dog will relieve himself to shed those few extra ounces!

You will also need to take advice as to which food supplements are beneficial for your breed.

With so many supplements in complete prepared canine foods these days, sometimes no supplements are recommended at all, as they can even be detrimental. There are many high-quality canine foods on the market today, so you will not be lacking in options when selecting a food for your own dog.

ALL-BREED DISQUALIFICATIONS

Spaying and castration are not the only disqualifications for pure-bred dogs in shows. Most breed standards list specific disqualifications for each breed, which are in addition to those that apply to all breeds. Dogs of any breed that are deaf, blind or lame, as well as dogs that have been altered by artificial means (other than those specified in the breed standard, such as tail docking and ear cropping) will be disqualified. Likewise, any corrective surgeries to the eyes, ears, mouth or nose are disqualifications, including surgeries for medical reasons such as cleft palate or harelip as well as hip dysplasia, patellar luxation and hernias. Dogs that have worn braces or bands or have had any dental restoration are also disqualified. Dogs whose coat colors have been altered or enhanced are also considered ineligible for competition. No dog that is showing signs of a communicable disease (or has suffered from such within 30 days of the show day) will be allowed on the show grounds.

Your dog's appearance is a reflection of your care, ability and devotion. If your dog doesn't look great, neither will you. This Bloodhound most assuredly is in good hands.

OFF TO THE SHOW

You will select the shows that you wish to enter via your country's dog press, kennel clubs and breed clubs, and you can usually obtain schedules for these shows directly from the hosting club(s). These things should be done well in advance of the shows. In most countries, the closing date for entries is several weeks before the show date; some even operate a sliding scale of fees so that the later you enter, the more you pay. Hence, be warned! Also be sure to fill out your entry forms carefully and correctly.

Shortly before the show, you will receive your entry passes in the mail, though this may vary in some countries. Check that the entries you receive are those you expect and that all details are correct. You will probably also receive a schedule of judging, indicating the time at which your breed will be judged, and the ring number. Take care that your breed's judging does not begin before the standard time for commencement of judging at this particular show. In some countries, this happens frequently when the number of exhibits in any one breed is espe-

cially high. If a plan of the show layout is included, it will be helpful to acquaint yourself with it before going to the show. It is remarkable how disoriented you can become with the excitement of arriving with your dogs while laden down with equipment.

Unless classes are for both sexes, dogs are generally judged before bitches. This means that if your breed is judged first in a given ring, and you have a young male, you will have to arrive at the show very early. This is especially so if you have a coated breed that will need to be freshly groomed right before your turn in the ring. In any event, regardless of breed, you will need to give your dog time to settle down and get a little lead exercise before entering the ring.

There are also cases in which there will be two judges officiating for your breed, one for dogs and one for bitches. This most likely means that dog and bitch judging will take place in different rings, so you will need to know for sure which is the correct ring for you. This also means that dog and bitch judging will take place simultaneously (not dogs

Off to the show! In their crates is the best way for dogs to travel; the crates also are useful for housing the dogs once you reach the show site.

before bitches), in which bitch judging will also commence at the beginning of the day (requiring the bitches to arrive early, too).

Leave ample time for your journey to the show, and make sure that any dogs you have left at home will be well taken care of in your absence. If you have more than one show dog, be sure that you are taking the right one to the show. To arrive with the wrong dog is very disappointing!

It is always wise to fill up your car's fuel tank the day before you leave, bearing in mind that you may well be starting off on your trip at the crack of dawn, before most gas stations are open. Pack your show bag in advance, too, and don't forget those all-important entry passes. You will need to carry water in the car for your dogs, and it is always wise to have a "space blanket" with you in case of hot weather. Such blan-

kets, which are silver on one side only, are usually obtainable at large shows and work wonders in expelling the heat. On a hot day, the blanket can be placed over a dog's traveling crate (silver side outermost) so that he does not get too hot during the journey. However, you will still have to check the dog regularly en route. Leave nothing to chance!

If you choose to feed your dog at the show, you will need to pack his food as well as his water. Many exhibitors, however, find that their dogs have little interest in food until they return home. Your own meals are also worthy of consideration beforehand. At some shows, usually those that are breed-specific, the hosting club offers very good food at reasonable prices. Selling such refreshments helps to raise money toward club funds, so it is always a nice gesture to support this if possible. However, at other shows, only professional catering is available; this can be extremely expensive, so you may decide to bring along a packed lunch.

It is surprising how your show costs will mount up. Apart from the entry fees, the cost of things like show catalogs, transportation, food, parking at the show site, etc., need to be taken into consideration. From the outset, you should never lose sight of the fact that dog showing is a costly hobby.

Provide for your dog's safety and comfort at the show site, especially outdoors in warm weather. This Soft Coated Wheaten Terrier has it made in the shade in his own ex-pen with protective cover.

Dog shows are wonderful social events where observing and meeting other fanciers are just as much fun as competing.

Upon arriving at the show, you first priority will be to get your dog settled in the appropriate place, but it is also wise to find out where the human restrooom facilities are located. It is usually wise to pay a visit at the beginning of the show, for lines often grow longer as the day progresses, and the last thing you want to do is miss your dog's class because you are waiting in the lavatory!

Depending on the country in which you live, your breed of dog and the type of show, you may find that your dog is benched while waiting for exhibition in the show ring. Benching varies somewhat from country to country. Often the bench is raised from the ground, but at some shows it is at floor level, always with partitions between dogs. Small dogs are generally kept in crates on their benches. Sometimes crates are provided by the show society, but usually the exhibitor brings them along to the show. Larger dogs are usually attached to their benches by a benching chain, but this also can differ according to the show. If your dog is attached by a benching chain, it is important to check the length of the chain so that your dog can neither get off the bench nor come to any harm. All dogs will appreciate their own bedding on the bench, so remember to bring this along from home. If you do not stay beside your dog throughout the show, it is important that you check on him regularly or, ideally, leave someone in charge to supervise him during your absence.

SHOW-SITE TIPS

Dogs need to be exercised at shows; exercise areas are often designated. Wherever your dog relieves himself, clean up after him immediately! All shows provide suitable receptacles to dispose of doggy droppings, and it is important that we dog lovers do not give the anti-dog lobby any cause for complaint! Incidentally, if your dog happens to "go" while in the exhibition ring, it is your duty to clean up after your dog, not the duty of the steward. There may be exceptions to this in certain countries, and sometimes stewards can be generous with their help in this regard, but the general rule is that every owner is responsible for cleaning up after his own dog. Should you fail to do so, you will not win favor with the other exhibitors or the officials.

How Best to Show

SELECTING CLASSES

When you fill out your entry form for a show, you will select the class or classes in which you want to enter your dog. You should pay careful attention when making your selections. Entering dogs in inappropriate classes is a fundamental error made by many novice exhibitors, so try not to fall into that trap.

In some countries, there is little choice as to which classes you enter; in other countries, the range is wide. There are classes based on age, and others in which

The Bergamasco is considered a rare breed in most places outside its homeland, Italy, and therefore may be entered in special classes for rare breeds or those not fully recognized by the governing kennel club, depending on where the show is held.

DON'T OVERDO IT!

Many new exhibitors feel compelled to enter a whole range of classes. Then, at the show, not only do they discover that this can be a little embarrassing but also that the puppy will tire easily if entered in too many classes. Something else to be warned against is entering your puppy at too many shows, especially during the early months of his life. It is all too easy for a dog of any age to become bored by the show scene, so don't be over-enthusiastic to the detriment of your dog's enjoyment.

eligibility is restricted to maximum wins. A prime example is in the UK, where even a six-month-old puppy that has never won anything is eligible to compete in every class up to and including the Open Class (but not the Veteran Class, which is for older dogs). On the other hand, a champion is only permitted to compete in the Open Class (unless an age class is appropriate). This means that it is possible to enter one's newcomer puppy in the same class as champions, against which he will be totally out of his league, being so immature.

AT THE SHOW

Unless your dog is entered in the very first class of the day, you will have an opportunity to watch exactly how the judge is conducting the ring. This can be invaluable. In the knowledge that your own dog is fully prepared for his entrance into the ring, take a few moments to study the ring and to watch how the judge is moving each exhibit. For example, is he requesting the handlers to gait the dogs in a triangle and just once up and down, or, after the triangle, is he watching them make their circuit back to the line of other exhibits? Does the judge show any preference as to the direction in which he requires the dogs to face while standing?

If it is a hot summer day, how can you protect your dog from the heat when the two of you are in the ring? You probably can provide him with shade by protecting him with your shadow but, in some breeds, people like to take damp towels into the ring to cool down their dogs. There are so many factors to consider, and a few moments' observation and contemplation by the ringside can certainly pay dividends.

You will also find that your ring number may be available before entry into the ring. It may be located on your bench or issued at the secretary's table; alternatively, numbers may be given out in the ring before judging of your class. If the number is available beforehand, never go into the ring without it or you will not be allowed to be judged until it is located. You must wear your number visibly, either by attaching it on an armband or with a ring clip. You are unlikely to find these at pet shops, but you will be able to purchase them at shows.

IN THE RING

At some shows and in some countries, exhibits are required to stand in numerical order. If not, you can carefully time your entry into the ring to gain a place in line that will suit your dog best. If you are new to the show ring, it is not generally a good idea to head the line, for you may feel more comfortable following someone else. If you know that your dog is a reluctant mover, placing your-

ENTER WITH CARE

When deciding on which class to enter your dog, male or female, you must carefully check the show schedule to make sure that you have selected the right class. Depending on the age of the dog, previous first-place wins and the sex of the dog, you must make the best choice.

self at the end of the line can be sensible so that you do not hold up anyone following you.

Another consideration is the size of your dog. If he is a little small for his age, try not to stand him next to a large exhibit; if your dog is larger than you would like, the reverse is true. In classes with dogs of different breeds, the judge usually requests that the steward arranges the dogs such that all "table" dogs head the line, and sometimes that all exhibits of a certain breed are grouped together. Should this not be the case, you would be wise to consider which dogs your own is next to, especially avoiding any that appear to overly dominant in presence.

As you observe and enter more shows, you will also become wise about which exhibitors are likely to chatter too much to their neighbors, and it would be prudent to give these people a wide berth. In the ring, you will need to give your dog your full concentration, without unnecessary distractions. Apart from focusing on your dog, your concentration must also be on the judge. Watch his every move and carry out his instructions to the letter. If the judge requests a triangle when you move, don't do a circle. The judge requests a certain pattern for a reason, so that he can watch your dog moving in specific directions. Nothing aggravates a judge more than an exhibitor who

does not pay attention to the directions given.

Keep an eye on the judge at all times. Although you may allow your dog to relax, take care that the judge is not looking your way when your dog decides to put his feet in an unflattering position. Many a judge casts a quick eye on a dog that has already been judged to compare the dog with another, often because he is mentally "placing" the dogs before the class draws to its conclusion.

When the judge is assessing the final exhibit in the class, you will need to stand your dog correctly, setting him off to his best advantage. The steward may, but not always, alert exhibitors that the last dog is being assessed, so you should always remain attentive and well prepared for the crucial moment of selection.

A judge may ask to see all or just a few of the exhibits move again, so listen carefully to instructions. The judge might also want to re-check certain points on

A huge class can be an intimidating sight to a novice exhibitor.

The dog must do more than just look great; he must move well, too. Proper gait means proper construction, so the judge watches each dog move to ensure that it has the typical gait for its breed.

followed by the second-place winner, and so on. Again, it is imperative that you pay close attention to the judge so that you don't miss your award.

Do not leave the ring unless requested to do so, as the judge and stewards will have certain documentation to complete. If a critique has not been written by the judge at the time of assessment, the winning dogs may also be asked to wait a while longer while this is done. Once again, this procedure varies from country to country.

Win or lose, always remember that your dog is very much more than just a show dog, so let him know that you love him dearly, no matter what happens in the ring! Enjoy the rest of your day at the show, learning by watching other exhibits in the ring.

your dog, so be prepared for this. Always keep in mind that your inexperienced youngster may not be familiar with a judge suddenly approaching him on the floor. It is important, at this early stage in your show-dog's career, that he has every confidence in you so that he does not become unsettled in the ring.

If the class is large, the judge may call out just a few exhibits before making a final selection, or he may make his placings directly from the full line-up of dogs. The number of placements will differ according to the show. In some countries, the prizewinners are brought into the center of the ring in reverse order of their placements (with the first-place dog being awarded last); in other countries, the first-place winner is

DO NOT SHOW

Showing a dog that is sick, lame or recovering from surgery or infection puts the dog under a tremendous amount of stress while putting other dogs at risk of contracting the illness, which is why dogs with any of these conditions likely will not be allowed at the show. Also, bitches in heat will distract the males who are competing, and bitches that are pregnant will be stressed and exhausted by a long day of showing, so it's inconsiderate to your bitch and to other exhibitors to show her during these times.

TEMPERAMENT, TOO!

Temperament in the show ring is just as important as physical conformation. Each dog should display the typical temperament for his breed, as detailed in the breed standard. Furthermore, an aggressive or fearful dog should not be shown, as bad behavior will not be tolerated and may pose a threat to the judge, other exhibitors, you and your dog. Obviously, your dog must be politely behaved around other dogs and around strangers.

What outshines a smartly presented Wire Fox Terrier! The dog is not the only one who should be looking his best in the ring. A neatly dressed handler, looking sharp but not conspicuous, accentuates the dog without drawing attention away from the dog.

YOUR OWN PRESENTATION AND ETIQUETTE

DRESSING FOR THE RING

It goes without saying that you have put much time, thought and effort into the selection of your show dog and his upbringing, care and training. Thus it also should go without saying that you will want to do him justice in the ring.

There is absolutely no logic in a dog that is turned out to perfection while his handler looks like a disheveled mess! While the most acceptable attire for you is likely to differ according to the breed you are showing, you will want to present yourself tidily whatever the breed. This much you owe to your dog.

If you are a lady, high-heeled stiletto shoes would be entirely inappropriate, in part because you may step on your own dog or, worse still, someone else's! You need comfortable shoes that allow you to move well when gaiting your dog for the judge's appraisal. Some exhibitors even go so far as to go barefoot in the ring, but you need not go to such extremes. I don't!

Avoid wearing a lot of dangling or showy jewelry that may distract your dog or perhaps

Always be gracious to the judge, no matter how he places your dog. You never know when you may meet in the ring again.

"TREAT" OTHERS WELL

If yours is a breed that traditionally demands tidbits in the ring, give some consideration to other exhibitors. Restrict the treats to your own dog only, please, and don't throw them too far away from your dog, for this can be very distracting to others.

complement your dog. If you have a black dog, it would be pointless to wear a black suit, for the dog's outline would be completely lost. Instead, wear a contrasting color that sets off your dog to perfection. Also keep in mind that if you wear one color on your lower half and a different color on top, both colors must complement his coat. Should you need to bend down with your dog to present him, neither color must conceal any of the dog's features.

Women should avoid wearing flouncy skirts that will not only flap in the dog's face while he is moving but also will hamper the judge's view of the dog—this is the very last thing you want to do! Gentlemen should remove any loose change from their pockets before going into the ring, because it will rattle and cause distraction.

RING ETIQUETTE

When standing your dog in line for the judge's appraisal at the beginning and end of a class, you clearly want your dog to look his best. In standing your dog, however, please don't overshadow someone else, for this will not be appreciated. You may, though, wish to consider the lie of the land or your dog's coat pattern. Although at some shows and in some countries dogs all have to face the same direction, sometimes it is permissible to stand them facing either direction. In the latter case, if you are in an outdoor

get caught in his coat. Also, try not to offend the judge and other exhibitors by wearing anything too revealing. It has to be said that some exhibitors select their outfits according to the judge, but this is really an insult to the judge concerned if a lady has chosen to wear a low neckline and tight pants!

Clothes should be comfortable, neat and tidy, and you should choose your outfit to ring and have ended up in a position where the ground slopes, it may be to your advantage to turn your dog around. Likewise, if your dog's coat pattern is more esthetically pleasing on one side of his body, you may want to turn him to show off his best side.

The position of the sun can also be something of a nightmare, especially for the judge. The sun glaring into a dog's eyes can understandably make him squint and can even artificially lighten the color of the eye, so that even a dark eye can appear paler than it actually is. This is another reason that you may wish to alter your dog's direction if this is permissible.

Some exhibitors will insist on taking their female dogs to shows when they are in season, but this is largely frowned upon. A bitch in season is most certainly a cause of distraction for the male dogs. Even if your bitch is not entered in a mixed-sex class, males may follow her into the ring and will try to follow her scent. This means that a male, especially if he is a stud dog, will not give his best performance through no fault of his own.

Whatever placing you have received, never show disgust in the ring. Gone are the days when exhibitors would tear up their award cards in front of the judge. Today such behavior usually carries a heavy penalty. Keep calm at all times, try never to show that

SHOW-RING ETIQUETTE

Just as with anything else, there is a certain etiquette to the show ring that can only be learned through experience. Showing your dog can be quite intimidating to you as a novice when it seems as if everyone else knows what they are doing. You can familiarize yourself with ring procedure beforehand by taking classes to prepare you and your dog for conformation showing and by talking with experienced handlers. When you are in the ring, it is very important to pay attention and listen to the instructions you are given about where to move your dog. Remember, even the most skilled handlers had to start somewhere. Keep it up and you too will become a proficient handler as you gain practice and experience.

you are overly disappointed not to have won and certainly don't complain publicly about the placements.

If you are placed, but not at the head of the line, it is generally considered polite to congratulate the winner briefly before leaving the ring. Always remember that if every judge had the same opinion, there would only ever be one winner! Your turn may come another day. After all, you decided to enter the show for that judge's opinion; if you didn't like the outcome, it is your prerogative not to enter under the same judge on another occasion.

Professional dog photographers know how to set up poses to highlight a dog's winning qualities. This Australian Terrier glistens as much as his silver cup.

RECORDING AND ADVERTISING YOUR WINS

RECORD-KEEPING

Keeping an accurate record of your dog's wins is important for various reasons. Often, wins count toward certain titles. In some countries dogs cannot be entered in particular classes, because they have won more than the specified number of prizes to be eligible for that class. This means that if you have entered your dog in a class lower than the one in which he should have competed, any prize won will subsequently be disallowed.

Some breed clubs also offer annual trophies that are awarded on a points system. This again is a good reason for keeping careful records, for it will be your own responsibility to submit your relevant wins if you wish to compete for such an award.

It would be sensible to buy a record book at one of your very first shows (record books may be difficult to find in pet stores). In it you can keep track of your losses as well as your wins. As time goes on, you will have compiled notes and will easily be able to see which judges liked your dog and which thought less

highly of him, a useful reference when you have the opportunity to go under a judge a second time around.

ADVERTISING

When your dog has had a good win, why not let everyone know about it? This will bring your dog to the attention of others—and keep in mind that some of the people who see the advertisement will be judges.

Advertising takes some preparation, so it is helpful to have a few good-quality photographs available for the time that your big win occurs. In every country, there is a handful of professional

Exhibitors know the value of having some good professional photos of their show dogs.

Photos in traditional dress make lovely pictures while highlighting the breed's origins. This is a Rafiero do Alentejo and handler at the World Dog Show.

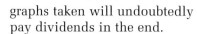

canine photographers who attend the shows and sell owners excellent-quality color prints for use in ads. If you choose the best, you will not be disappointed. The initial cost of having good photographs taken will undoubtedly pay dividends in the end.

Keep in mind that your dog will not always look as he did when at the peak of his show career. If you obtain a few top-quality photos when he is looking his very best, you will be able to treasure them for many years to come. You may have a breed that shows considerable change in coat throughout the year, so you will have to consider this when planning your photo shoot so that the shots are taken when the coat is in peak condition.

Don't rush into advertising when your win is not a particularly high one. A third-place award in a mediocre class may be thrilling to win, but the news is not worthy of hitting the headlines. Wait until your dog has done something really special,

This is no pose! This Junior Handler is genuinely beaming from ear to ear over her success with her Pomeranian.

BE PHOTOGENIC
Too many exhibitors effectively waste money on their ads by including inferior photographs, such as a snapshot taken in the back yard with the dog ungroomed and not standing correctly. Let's face it, you don't want people to look at a photo of your dog and comment, "How in the world did that one win?" This will do considerably more harm than good.

Of course, a win shot from a show makes a wonderful advertisement. The specialty dog-show magazines are full of photos of dogs on the winner's stand.

This is how a winner's day ends, getting primped for his victory photo. The crowd loves to see a big dog like the Newfoundland take home the Best-in-Show ribbon.

such as a particularly significant win or perhaps a run of successes.

You will need to decide where to advertise, for there are many options. The weekly canine press is always worthwhile, for it is here that your advertisement will be viewed by the widest audience. Should you wish to capture interest within the fraternity of your own breed, you may choose to advertise in a breed-specific publication. Most clubs have their own special publications, often issued on a quarterly or annual basis. It is usually less expensive to advertise in a club publication than in an all-breed publication with wider circulation. These days many club publications are very high-quality, offering both black and white and color options.

When advertising, you should also consider publications that

A Best Puppy win and a bright future ahead! This Chinese Crested poses with the elegance of a thoroughbred racehorse.

come out only on an annual basis, usually toward the close of the year. Many leading canine newspapers also issue special annual editions. These are often very extensive issues and are eagerly read and absorbed by dog lovers for months, even years, following their issue date. In such publications, your aim will be merely to promote your show dogs and, if you are breeding, your kennel. This type of ad will therefore have quite a different emphasis from an ad in a weekly issue, for the latter will highlight a specific win that took place perhaps the previous week.

If you enjoy showing your dog, you will surely enjoy your wins. Hopefully these will be only the beginning of great successes to follow in the years ahead.

CALENDAR DOG

Sometimes breed clubs publish calendars with photographs of dogs printed on each page. These pages are "sold" to advertisers who wish their dogs to be featured. This is a good idea and (if not a private enterprise) a great way of raising money for the club. However, before deciding where to spend the money you have allocated for advertising, do consider the spectrum of readership. Ask yourself how many people will see your ad and who those people will be.

Many breed clubs like to hold their specialty shows outdoors in temperate weather-months, providing a nice opportunity for breed fanciers from across the country to gather with their dogs, usually for an event that lasts a few days.

SHOWING IN THE UNITED STATES

BY ANN HEARN

Dog shows in the United States are very much like dog events all over the world. Americans on the show scene have the same intense competitive spirit, the determination to breed better and better and the enjoyable desire to acquire friends throughout the world who have the same interests.

American exhibitors, breeders and judges are firmly focused on family participation. This hobby offers many benefits for families, and the American Kennel Club (AKC) creates an opportunity for and encourages involvement. A family that takes part in all aspects of the dog sport is inevitably embraced in togetherness. Showing teaches patience, the win/lose facts of life and the responsibility of caring for a living thing; it also provides children with the opportunity to meet other young people with similar interests.

The sport provides competition while teaching participants about companionship, independence, self-value and cordiality. All of these skills are necessities for success in everyday life. It has

TOMORROW'S SHOWFOLK

For budding dog handlers, ages 10 to 18 years, Junior Showmanship provides an excellent training ground for the next generation of dog professionals. Owning and caring for a dog are wonderful methods of teaching children responsibility, and Junior Showmanship builds upon that foundation. Juniors learn by grooming, handling and training their dogs, and the quality of a Junior's presentation of the dog (and himself) is evaluated by a licensed judge. The Junior can enter with any registered AKC dog to compete, including an ILP, provided that the dog lives with him or a member of his family.

Junior Showmanship competitions are divided into two classes: Novice (for beginners) and Open (for Juniors who have three first-place wins in the Novice Class). The Junior must run with the dog with the rest of the handlers and dogs, stack the dog for examination and individually gait the dog in a specific pattern. Juniors should practice with a handling class or an experienced handler before entering the Novice Class so that they recognize all of the jargon that the judge may use.

A National Junior Organization was founded in 1997 to help promote the sport of dog showing among young people. The AKC also offers a Junior Scholarship for Juniors who excel in the program.

also been observed that focusing on a mutual goal increases a family's enjoyment of life.

JUNIOR SHOWMANSHIP

The American Kennel Club offers many awards and incentives for the junior showman—from qualifying for national competition to public recognition for top placements. The AKC now recognizes Juniors who participate in all events, not just conformation. Juniors who handle a dog to a title in obedience, agility or any of the performance events will receive a certificate as well as a pin with a bar for each title. Juniors are encouraged to do as much with their dogs as is possible for their breed. Juniors have successfully handled their dogs to eligibility for participation in the prestigious Obedience Invitational and Agility Tournament. AKC Juniors are encouraged to become the positive future of dog shows and breeding programs. As such, professional handlers provide training within their kennels and at show sites for our young people.

To participate in AKC events, each Junior must obtain a Junior number. This allows AKC to track their participation. Each Junior receives the *Junior Newsletter*, which is sent three times a year. The AKC and the AKC Registered Handlers Program offer seminars for Juniors in conjunction with different club show clusters. These seminars vary from get-togethers with informational updates and in-ring practice to all-day programs that offer varied topics. Canine Good Citizen (CGC) tests often are offered in conjunction with these seminars as a way to further develop and emphasize responsible dog ownership.

The AKC offers scholarships to those individuals who have participated in our sport and who attend accredited schools. The first year in which scholarships were offered, 1996, there was $5,000 to distribute; this figure jumped to $100,000 in 2003. Many all-breed kennel clubs match the scholarship funds, which has been a wonderful additional source of assistance for our Juniors.

The AKC encourages national parent clubs, all-breed clubs and specialty clubs to support and acknowledge the Juniors, as they are the future of the sport!

A visit to a dog show might just be the spark that a dog-loving youngster needs to become interested in showing herself. Many shows welcome canine spectators, too!

SCHOLARSHIP OPPORTUNITY

The AKC offers a Junior competition at the AKC/Eukanuba Invitational. To be eligible to compete, the Junior must have five wins in the Open Class with competition and have a 3.0 grade point average or equivalent in school. The dog community is very pleased with the positive results, as almost 90 Juniors received invitations to compete in a recent show. The prizes for this competition are scholarships offered by the Eukanuba Company.

MEET THE AKC

The American Kennel Club was established in 1884 to promote the study, breeding, exhibiting and advancement of pure-bred dogs, and to become the registering body for all pure-bred dogs. It is the largest non-profit pure-bred dog registry in the United States. AKC registration means that a dog, as well as the dog's parents and ancestors, are pure-bred. Dogs must be of an AKC-recognized breed, be registered and have an

Handlers sometimes go to great lengths to set up their dogs in the correct position—the Bulldog on the far left needs a little bit of encouragement!

AKC registration number to be able to compete in AKC events.

The American Kennel Club offers the opportunity and encouragement to breed better dogs. Breeders prove their stock to be worthy and correct according to the breed standard as the dogs compete for awards on the breed level, the group level and the all-breed level. This is a triple method of proving your efforts as a breeder and the worthiness of your dog!

AKC CLASSES

Let's start by examining the different classes at shows. In each breed of dog, males are judged first, then bitches. There are six classes for each sex:

• Puppy: For dogs between 6 months and one year of age. This class may be broken down into 6–9 months old and 9–12 months old in two separate classes;

• Dogs of 12–18 months of age;

DEFINING THE STANDARD

The American Kennel Club defines a standard as: "A description of the ideal dog of each recognized breed, to serve as an ideal against which dogs are judged at shows." Furthermore, the picture that the standard draws of the dog's type, gait, temperament and structure is the guiding image used by breeders as they plan their programs. A breed's parent club creates and approves the standard, which then goes on to the AKC for approval. The AKC states that "An understanding of any breed must begin with its standard. This applies to all dogs, not just those intended for showing."

The cream of the crop for each breed is represented at the annual Westminster Kennel Club show, aptly demonstrated by this lineup of lovely Yorkshire Terriers.

• Novice: For dogs that have never won a first placement;
• Bred-by-Exhibitor: For all dogs except champions, six months of age and over, that are on the day of the show owned and exhibited by the person or kennel who is the registered breeder;
• American-bred: For dogs born in the US;
• Open: For all dogs/bitches.
It is generally felt that the more experienced dogs will be found in the Open and American-bred classes. However, the Bred-by-Exhibitor class is the exhibitors' way of showing off their efforts and stating their faith in their exhibits.

After the classes for the males have been judged in a given breed, the winners of each class continue to compete in the Winners Class.

Two awards are given in the Winners Class: a Winners and a Reserve Winners if the competition is sufficient and the quality is justified. This procedure is then repeated for the bitches. A judge has the right to withhold any ribbon offered if the exhibit(s) are not worthy.

The six aforementioned classes are for non-champions of record. Best of Breed competition is for all champions in the given breed entered on that day (both dogs and bitches) and the Winners Dog and Winners Bitch. From this group, one is selected for Best of Breed (male or female). A Best of (the two) Winners (dog or bitch) is selected and a Best of Opposite Sex winner is selected from the remaining exhibits that are the opposite sex to the Best of Breed

Representatives of the AKC's Non-Sporting Group (Dalmatian) and Herding Group (Old English Sheepdog), two of the seven breed groups.

"Champion" is added as a title at the beginning of the dog's registered name, i.e., Champion (abbreviated Ch.) Darlings Rusty Spot.

HOW AN ALL-BREED SHOW IS ORGANIZED

The show frequently begins with the national anthem, after which the first class enters the ring. This will be the 6- to 9-month-old males of a given breed. Should there be no entries in a class, the judging will start with the first class with entries. There is no limit to the number of dogs allowed to be shown and entered. The judge will select first, second, third and fourth placements and will present a ribbon to each selected dog. The color of the ribbon denotes the placement received: blue for first, red for second, yellow for third and white for fourth. All dogs that were not given a placement leave the ring while the judge marks his judge's books, indicating the winners.

The next class (9- to 12-month-old males) will come into the ring, and the same procedure

(BoB) winner. The BoB winner will then go on to further competition later in the day with other dogs in his Group.

Championship points can be won by one dog and one bitch in each breed at any show, providing there are sufficient entries. To earn the title of Champion, a dog is required to win 15 points, with 2 major wins under different judges with a minimum of 3 points and a maximum of 5 points. Championship status is maintained for life, and the word

AKC GROUPS

For showing purposes, the American Kennel Club divides its recognized breeds into seven groups: Sporting Dogs, Hounds, Working Dogs, Terriers, Toys, Non-Sporting Dogs and Herding Dogs.

The hope of each exhibitor is that his dog will end the day behind one of these signs!

occurs. This process continues until all six classes have been judged in the order in which the classes were listed previously. The winners of each class, a possible six in all, will come back into the ring and compete for Winners Dog. The Winners Dog, then, is the best on that day of the non-champion males entered and shown.

The Winners Dog and Winners Bitch are those that are awarded points. The number of males entered determines how many points the Winners Dog receives toward his championship; likewise, the number of females determines how many points the Winners Bitch will receive. The AKC maintains a record of each dog's wins.

A Reserve Winners Dog and Bitch are also selected as back-ups for the available points, should the winners become ineligible for the award. Reasons for ineligibility include the dog's being entered incorrectly, AKC registry paperwork that does not correspond with the entry information or even the wrong dog's being exhibited by mistake. As strange as that may

SPECIAL AWARDS

A show-giving club's members frequently wish to make contributions, in addition to the official ribbon, to a dog's win. Prior to the publication of the show's announcement in the Premium List, which is mailed to all exhibitors in the show's area and those judges involved, trophy donations can be made for any win from a Puppy Class win to a Best of Breed win. These trophies can be dog-related or not. It is merely a way of expressing the donor's appreciation of the entries at that show.

AMERICAN KENNEL CLUB TITLES

The AKC offers over 40 different titles to dogs in competition. Depending on the events that your dog can enter, different titles apply. Some titles can be applied as prefixes, meaning that they are placed before the dog's name (e.g., Ch. King of the Road) and others are used as suffixes, placed after the dog's name (e.g., King of the Road, CD). Here are some of the common titles

These titles are used as suffixes:

Obedience
- CD (Companion Dog)
- CDX (Companion Dog Excellent)
- UD (Utility Dog)
- UDX (Utility Dog Excellent)
- VCD1 (Versatile Companion Dog 1)
- VCD2 (Versatile Companion Dog 2)
- VCD3 (Versatile Companion Dog 3)
- VCD4 (Versatile Companion Dog 4)

Tracking Tests
- TD (Tracking Dog)
- TDX (Tracking Dog Excellent)
- VST (Variable Surface Tracker)

Agility Trials
- NA (Novice Agility)
- OA (Open Agility)
- AX (Agility Excellent)
- MX (Master Agility Excellent)
- NAJ (Novice Jumper with Weaves)
- OAJ (Open Jumper with Weaves)
- AXJ (Excellent Jumper with Weaves)
- MXJ (Master Excellent Jumper with Weaves)

Hunting Test
- JH (Junior Hunter)
- SH (Senior Hunter)
- MH (Master Hunter)

Herding Test
- HT (Herding Tested)
- PT (Pre-Trial Tested)
- HS (Herding Started)
- HI (Herding Intermediate)
- HX (Herding Excellent)

Lure Coursing
- JC (Junior Courser)
- SC (Senior Courser)
- MC (Master Courser)

Earthdog
- JE (Junior Earthdog)
- SE (Senior Earthdog)
- ME (Master Earthdog)

These titles are used as prefixes:

Conformation Dog Shows
- Ch. (Champion)

Obedience Trials
- NOC (National Obedience Champion)
- OTCH (Obedience Trial Champion)
- VCCH (Versatile Companion Champion)

Tracking Tests
- CT [Champion Tracker (TD, TDX and VST)]

Agility Trials
- MACH (Master Agility Champion)
- MACH2, MACH3, MACH4, etc.

Field Trials
- FC (Field Champion)
- AFC (Amateur Field Champion)
- NFC (National Field Champion)
- NAFC (National Amateur Field Champion)
- NGDC (National Gun Dog Champion)
- NOGDC (National Open Gun Dog Champion)
- GDSC (Gun Dog Stake Champion)
- RGDSC (Retrieving Gun Dog Stake Champion)

Herding Trials
- HC (Herding Champion)

Dual
- DC (Dual Champion — Ch. and FC)

Triple
- TC (Triple Champion — Ch., FC and OTCH)

Coonhounds
- NCH (Nite Champion)
- GNCH (Grand Nite Champion)
- SHNCH (Senior Grand Nite Champion)
- SGCH (Senior Grand Champion)
- GFC (Grand Field Champion)
- SGFC (Senior Grand Field Champion)
- WCH (Water Race Champion)
- GWCH (Grand Water Race Champion)
- SGWCH (Senior Grand Water Race Champion)

sound, it has happened inadvertently. Also, the Reserve award is an excellent recognition of a dog's quality and states by virtue of the win that, had the Winners Dog (or Bitch) not been at the show, the Reserve was next in line to receive the win.

Upon completion of judging the males, the same procedures take place for the bitches. After all of these classes have been judged, and a Winners Dog and Winners Bitch have been selected, the competition moves to a higher and more competitive level with the Best of Breed competition. The champions of record enter the ring along with the Winners Dog and Winners Bitch. From this group of dogs, a Best of Breed, a Best of Winners and a Best of Opposite Sex must be selected, in that order. The award for Best of Breed is a purple-and-gold ribbon, the Best of Winners receives a blue-and-white ribbon and the Best of Opposite Sex wins a red-and-white ribbon.

All winners of that breed are then excused from further judging except the Best of Breed winner, who will compete further. After all of the breeds at the show have gone through the same judging procedure and one dog is selected as Best of Breed from each breed, all of the day's Best of Breed winners come back for competition within their group. The judge will again examine each dog, and

select first- through fourth-place winners (known as Group 1, 2, 3 and 4). The ribbons are the same color for a class win, but are in a rosette fashion.

After all seven groups have been judged, the first-place dog from each of the groups will come back into the ring for Best in Show. The seven dogs are judged again, and the first-place winner, Best in Show, is awarded a large and impressive red, white and blue rosette.

Statisticians keep records of the number of dogs that each dog defeats at each show, as these totals could lead to future recognition as one of the year's top winners. The year's superlative top-winning dogs are recognized during the Westminster Kennel Club show, held annually in February. The honors bestowed upon the breeder(s), owner(s) and handler of the top dog are both generous and gratifying.

A wallful of accomplishments is the result of years of practice, dedication and true devotion to dogs and the sport of showing.

In a large class, such as this group of Weimaraners, it is more difficult to win points, as there are more dogs to defeat. The point system is based on many variables, including number of dogs, region of the country and overall popularity of breed.

CHAMPIONSHIP POINTS

Championship points are determined according to a point schedule based on specific zones of the country as designated by the AKC. The point schedule can differ from zone to zone and from breed to breed. The number of points allowed in each zone depends on how many dogs of each breed were entered in the previous year.

A single entry in a breed does not provide championship points, as at least one dog must be defeated to qualify for points. For example, if a puppy dog is the only class dog entered and shown, and he defeats a champion entered, he will win a point if the point schedule allows. Depending on the zone, the number of dogs defeated to qualify for points varies. Therefore, a dog could be shown in one area and only need to defeat one dog for points; in another area, the requirement for

dogs defeated will be higher, and a defeat of only one dog may not earn points.

As previously stated, it takes 15 points to make up an AKC champion. These wins must meet certain criteria. Two of the wins must be "major" wins of three to five points, under two different judges. The remainder of the points may come from single points with wins under different judges from those who awarded the major wins. A dog who wins all of his points with three major wins (five points per win) is considered a high-quality representative of the breed.

WHAT IS THE AKC?

The American Kennel Club (AKC) is the main governing body of the dog sport in the United States. Founded in 1884, the AKC consists of 500 or more independent dog clubs plus 4,500 affiliate clubs, all of which follow the AKC rules and regulations. The AKC maintains a registry for pure-bred dogs in the US and works to preserve the integrity of the sport and its continuation in the country. Over 1,000,000 dogs are registered each year, representing about 150 fully recognized breeds. Over 2,000,000 dogs enter to participate in the thousands of events held each year; in addition to conformation showing, the AKC offers a wide range of non-conformation and performance events.

CHARTING A CHAMPION'S COURSE

We'll plot the journey toward a championship with the example of our Bichon Frise, Nero, during his show career. Let's start his show career in Georgia, at an all-breed show in the Puppy Class. He wins his class only. He gets no points for that day. The next day, still in Georgia, he again

wins his class and goes on to Winners Dog. There are only two non-champion dogs (males) entered that day, and Nero defeats the other male. He receives one point as determined by the division in which he is shown, his breed and the number of non-champion dogs defeated.

The following weekend, we take Nero to North Carolina and again go Winners Dog as well as Best of Winners. More dogs are required to make up the points offered in North Carolina. At this show, there are more bitches entered and shown than dogs, and the points awarded for Winners Bitch was a major for three points. Even though there were only two points awarded in the dog classes, by going Best of Winners, Nero wins the same amount of points as the Winners Bitch. He now has his first major, plus the single point

It takes a true canine good citizen to behave well around the sights, sounds and smells of a dog show, but most show dogs become pros at the routine. It's just another day at the show for this Basset Hound.

AKC ZONES

The US is divided into 14 zones or divisions:

1. Connecticut, Maine, Massachusetts, New Hampshire, New York, Rhode Island, Vermont;
2. Delaware, New Jersey, Pennsylvania;
3. District of Columbia, Kentucky, Maryland, North Carolina, Tennessee, Virginia, West Virginia;
4. Alabama, Arkansas, Georgia, Louisiana, Mississippi, South Carolina;
5. Illinois, Indiana, Michigan, Ohio;
6. Iowa, Kansas, Minnesota, Missouri, Nebraska, Wisconsin;
7. Arizona, New Mexico, Oklahoma, Texas;
8. Colorado, Idaho, Nevada, Oregon, Utah, Washington, Wyoming;
9. California;
10. Alaska;
11. Hawaii;
12. Puerto Rico;
13. Montana, North Dakota, South Dakota;
14. Florida.

from the Georgia show, which gives him a total of four points toward his championship.

The same thing occurs on the next two days of the three-day show circuit. However, because the dogs actually brought into the ring changed due to an absent dog that had been shown on the previous days, the three-point major on Sunday is down to two single points. But Nero has both of his majors, plus three points, for a total of nine points. He is then taken to the Bichon National Specialty in California, a show for the Bichon breed only, and entered in the Bred-by-Exhibitor class. This is a class that a breeder enters to make sure his fellow Bichon friends and the judge recognize the quality of his efforts in breeding better dogs. A win at a National Specialty is considered the peak of recognition and respect, and is highly regarded among one's peers. And, from the Bred-by-Exhibitor class, the win takes on even more stature.

To take Winners at a specialty show is always a major win, especially since California requires more dogs for points. People from all over the world attend and show their Bichons; thus the large entries. The United States does not require a quarantine period for dogs being imported from other countries. Therefore a dog could fly into the US from Europe a week before the show and be shown at the specialty. If the paperwork with the AKC is handled in a timely fashion, a special registry number will be assigned to the dog. It is not likely the dog will return to his country soon after, as most countries do require a three- to six-month quarantine upon return.

But back to Nero at his National Specialty. He wins the Bred-by-Exhibitor class and, still showing great, wins Winners Dog

Maintaining a show dog in peak physical condition, healthy, fit and with a gleaming coat, is no small task, but the challenge of attaining a championship is certainly an exciting pursuit for those who love pure-bred dogs.

for the five-point major win. He now has more than enough major wins, with a total of 14 points. He is only one point away from his championship! The next two days, there are two all-breed shows in the area. Again Nero garners the award, and he goes home a champion with five major wins and several single points, which put him over the top for his championship. This is now signified by the title of Ch. before his registered name.

It is now time to celebrate and plan Nero's future. Will he continue to be shown in the Best of Breed classes as a champion and try for top-winning Bichon dog recognition, will he be used for stud purposes or will he return to the comfort of his home with nothing more to do than be a wonderful companion to his family? With time, he can do all of these things. A dog can continue to compete to become a top winner in his breed or among all breeds by winning many Best-in-Show awards. With judicious care, the dog can help improve and upgrade his breed by being bred to various quality bitches. Then, after his time as a heavy top competitor, he can retire to his home life. A dog's lifetime in the pinnacle of success can vary from only a year to a span of four or five years. After that, the dog becomes bored with the road, shows and required performance. At that point, it is better to withdraw from the show scene and enjoy your dog as a pet with the successes you have earned.

AKC GROUPS

AKC-recognized breeds are divided into seven groups, designated by the American Kennel Club, grouping together breeds with like purposes. The Sporting Group includes the gun dogs, retrieving dogs, flushing dogs and any other breeds that are intended to help put meat on the hunter's table. Within the Hound Group are two categories: the sighthounds and the scenthounds. These breeds are used for hunting game as well as for searching for items or persons. The Working Group consists of breeds designed for guarding both people and territories. The Terrier Group comprises the eradicators of unwanted critters, such as rats, rodents, foxes, etc. The Toy Group

WHAT'S ILP?
If you have acquired a puppy and have no interest in showing or breeding, you can apply for an ILP or an Indefinite Listing Privilege, which affords your dog the opportunity to participate in obedience, agility, tracking and many other performance events. An ILP does not replace the dog's registration certification, and all ILPs must belong to an AKC-recognized breed and be spayed or neutered.

contains the small breeds that offer companionship, which is very fulfilling to their owners. The Non-Sporting Group is the only group that has a kaleidoscope of different breeds that provide various functions, from bull-baiters, companion dogs and water dogs to barge guarders, fire-truck assistants and more. The Herding Group classifies those breeds with a natural instinct and skill for gathering together other animals. Interestingly, dogs of this group have also been observed herding children together to protect them from danger.

In show competition, the Best of Breed winners from each breed compete with all of the other Best of Breed winners in their designated group. After the winner of each group (Group 1) has been selected, there will be those seven group winners to come back into the ring to compete for Best in Show. As the levels progress, the competition gets tougher and the excitement and tension grow. Exhibits are applauded by the ringside as the judge goes over each dog. And no matter how large or small the show, Best in Show is still the most prestigious win.

There is also a Miscellaneous Group. Breeds that are undergoing the AKC acceptance process are temporarily held in this group while AKC recognition is justified, giving the breed full recognition and eligibility for championship

points. These breeds change frequently as each is recognized by the AKC and placed in the appropriate breed group. Competition for Miscellaneous breeds is solely within the Miscellaneous Group and on the breed level.

From the tallest of the hounds to the tiny toys, you'll see them all at an AKC all-breed show.

The Australian Shepherd is a natural beauty and popular showman, consistently drawing large entries at shows. These dogs are being judged at the prestigious Westminster show.

SHOW PROCEDURE

There are three types of conformation dog shows: all-breed shows, for all breeds approved by the American Kennel Club; specialty shows, for a single breed or variety; and group shows, for only those breeds in a certain group. A Best in Show is selected at all three types. The size of a show can be as large as 3,000 entered dogs or more, or as small as a single rare breed with very few registered and entered dogs.

Spayed or neutered dogs are not eligible to compete in conformation shows due to the "altering" of the entry. Altering a dog in any way, including any attempt to change the natural look of a dog, is not acceptable in AKC conformation shows, as this is not being honest. Some of the things that are against regulations are correcting a dog's incorrect occlusion, coloring a coat or pigmentation, surgically restructuring a tail or ears and other enhancements that do not give a true picture of the animal. These "hidden" things may adversely affect the ability to successfully select the best dogs for breeding programs.

At an official AKC all-breed show, the day begins fairly early. The entry for your dog to compete in a show must be in the office of the show's superintendent by a given deadline. A superintendent is an organization approved and licensed by the AKC to provide the paperwork, ribbons, judges' materials, armbands, ring stanchions and entry affirmation for a club's show. The superintendent is hired by the club that is holding the show, and the superintendent must adhere to the club's decisions as long as there is no conflict with AKC regulations. There are quite a few AKC-licensed superintendent companies available to assist in putting on a show.

Approximately six weeks prior to the show, the superintendent mails a premium list to the mailing list of active AKC exhibitors and judges. The premium list provides all of the pertinent information required for entering an exhibit in the show, including an official entry form, judges' list, date and location of show. There is a deadline for entry submission.

A judging schedule is mailed out at least a week prior to the show to all exhibitors and judges hired for the show. This schedule states the times at which each breed is to be shown. It is up to the exhibitor to have his dog at ringside at the appropriate time. Dogs must be clean, healthy and groomed according to the coat requirements for their breed. Grooming and physical condition are big parts of presenting your dog. No judge wants to examine a dog that is matted, has an offensive odor or is out of condition (too thin, too fat, no muscle tone, etc.)

An AKC judge must be at the show site a minimum of 30 minutes prior to judging. Obedience judges must be there more than 30 minutes prior. Conformation judges must regard their ring, establish where the examining table or ramp will be, if required, and provide the ring steward with the procedures they will utilize during the day. They will check their judges' books and have them ready and open to the page of the first breed of dog to be exhibited.

Frequently the show-giving club will begin the show by playing the national anthem, after which the ring steward will call the class into the ring. It is up to the judge to verify that the armband numbers of the exhibitors match those printed in the judge's book.

The same method is used all over the world to evaluate dogs physically. The judge needs to review the overall dog to determine if his balance is correct according to the standard. The judge must put his hands on the dog to check for proper bite, facial and head features, shoulder layback, coat texture, topline and muscle tone.

The judge checks all male dogs to be certain that both testicles are present and fully descended. Other things such as correct eye color and coat color are determined. By having each dog gait away from and back toward him, the judge is able to properly observe and assess movement. While moving, the dog must place his feet in the manner prescribed in the standard for that given breed. Having the dogs gait around the perimeter of the ring allows the judge to see the side movement, the reach and drive of the legs, the topline movement and the head carriage.

After reviewing all of the dogs in the class, with the framework of the breed's requirements and faults in mind, the judge is able to make his choices for first, second, third and fourth place. If he feels that there are no dogs in the class that are worthy of becoming champions, the judge may withhold any award he wishes. Should he decide to withhold first place, there will be no winner in that class. If a dog must be disqualified or excused for any reason, the points awarded are affected. The available points are lowered with each dog that must leave the ring without being judged.

TO CONTACT THE AKC

American Kennel Club
5580 Centerview Dr., Raleigh, NC
27606-3390 US
www.akc.org

Herding breeds, bright and athletic, consistently fare well in obedience competition. This Shetland Sheepdog demonstrates an off-lead heel, which is a required exercise in advanced levels of obedience.

how accomplished the child is. Should the dog feel the child is being threatened by another dog or person, and feels the need to protect the youngster, it would be physically impossible for the child to control a dog who outweighs him by 50 to 100 pounds.

After making his selection of first through fourth place, the judge returns to his official judge's book and marks his placements after verifying once again the correct armband numbers. A good ring steward will do the same in the ring steward's book. This provides back-up documentation should a question arise later. At the completion of the breeds to be judged that are listed in the judge's book, the judge must turn the signed book in to the show superintendent.

Judges are given a 30-minute to 1-hour lunch break, and the show-giving club provides the

While this may sound harsh, it is an excellent method of aiding the breeder in continuing to maintain the requirements set forth by the breed standard. Here are several reasons for withholding a ribbon (or ribbons): the dog(s) are not worthy of championship points; the judge is unable to physically examine the dog due to mismanagement by the handler, the dog's fear and/or illness (a dog must be excused if he becomes lame while in the ring); the dog attempts to bite or acts aggressively in any manner toward the judge, handler or other dogs.

The safety of the people and dogs at the dog show must be considered at all times. Sending a six-year-old child into the ring to exhibit a large dog such as a Bullmastiff is not wise, no matter

NON-CONFORMATION COMPETITION

In addition to conformation showing, the American Kennel Club offers non-conformation trials and performance events: obedience, agility, rally, lure coursing, tracking, Canine Good Citizen tests, field trials, hunting tests, herding trials, tracking tests, coonhound events and earthdog events. These events may be held in conjunction with a conformation show or may be held independently.

food and a place to sit down and relax. This is frequently a time for judges to discuss technical situations that they wish to have reviewed. Frequently, the AKC representative sits with them and is available for technical advice.

The American Kennel Club employs men and women as representatives to attend all shows around the country to assist the show-giving club, aid the judges and represent the AKC. Their days are strenuous and long, and require a great deal of diplomacy. A report on the show is generated immediately by the representative and submitted via Internet directly to the AKC. This report will cover all subjects regarding the show site, club involvement and behaviors, superintendent responses and responsibility,

judging questions, interviews with judges, observations, any issues that occurred requiring a Bench Show Committee decision and all of the Group placements and Best in Show. In fact, a representative may, by the end of the day, have done or been involved with anything at all that is part of the show to assure that all functions smoothly.

A Bench Show Committee is composed of the officers and directors of the show-giving club and the AKC representative for that show. This body must act in a disciplinary manner for disturbances at the show. Poor sportsmanship, mistreatment of dogs and abusive behavior and language are some of the problems that can require a Bench Show Committee hearing. It is the

Judges work hard at shows! Here, during Basenji judging, the judge moves down the line while the handlers stack their dogs in anticipation of their evaluation.

The judge assesses the dog's gait from the side and also watches the dog coming and going. Here's a sprightly Flat-Coated Retriever showing his stuff.

committee's task to make a suggestion to the AKC to take disciplinary steps against the individual(s) for their actions. The individuals involved in the situation are given the opportunity to state their sides and justify their actions against the charges. The AKC has the option to punish the individual with a fine, suspension from AKC functions for a specified time or lifetime suspension, or all of these things. These are serious situations and penalties that all parties involved wish to avoid.

BECOMING A JUDGE
The judge becomes knowledgeable about each breed's requirements and faults through in-depth study and observation, attending educational classes about each breed and taking written and verbal tests. A potential judge must justify to the AKC why he should be allowed to judge that breed.

Persons interested in becoming American Kennel Club-approved dog-show judges agree to abide by the AKC rules, to be professional at all times, to provide proof of their knowledge of the breeds they wish to adjudicate and to be recognized by the show-giving clubs as viable judges.

Becoming an AKC judge is not a simple matter. There are many requirements prescribed by the AKC that will prove, without a doubt, the judge's ability to main-

tain the standard of each breed judged, which will hopefully keep the breed in line with its official written description. The AKC provides a *Judges' Newsletter* quarterly to approved judges with current information, elements for discussion, notices about upcoming seminars and general helpful hints. The AKC makes a strong attempt to provide as much support to its judges as possible.

A new judge applicant must have certain credentials before requesting approval to judge. He must have bred, championed and been involved in a breed (or breeds) for 12 years, bred at least five litters and championed at least four dogs of his breeding. He must ring steward, judge matches and sweepstakes, take written tests on breed criteria and anatomy and then have a verbal interview with an AKC representative. All requirements must be written, provable and thorough. The potential judge must meet all of these requirements for each breed for which he is applying to judge.

Once approved to judge, the new judge must judge the breeds for which he is approved at least five times, with the AKC representative providing a written report on his judging abilities, correct placements, ring procedures and ring control. The new judge may then request permanent status for those breeds. The judge may then

JUDGES' ASSOCIATIONS

There are three judges' associations available for membership to all judges of record. They are Dog Judges of America, Inc., Senior Conformation Judges of America, Inc. and American Dog Show Judges, Inc. A judge may belong to none or any number of these groups. These associations offer educational programs, a voice for the judging community and an opportunity to discuss with fellow members any subject relating to judging.

study institutes; judging matches; mentoring with recognized breeders; in-ring observations with knowledgeable breeder-judges; written tests; a personal interview with an AKC representative; endorsement by the AKC in-house staff and, finally, approval by the AKC Board of Directors. No more than 13 breeds may be applied for at one time, and usually fewer are granted. A year must elapse between the last Board approval and the submission of the application for additional breeds.

Upon becoming approved for one complete group, a judge may apply to be approved to judge Best in Show. Approval to judge Junior Showmanship may be included on any application. Now that you've learned about the process, you can see why it has laughingly been expressed that it is easier to become a brain surgeon than an AKC dog-show judge!

The life of a judge takes on a "gypsy" air! When a judge accepts an assignment for a show, it could take him just about anywhere in the US. Paperwork must be exchanged with the hiring club, and a contract must be agreed upon and signed by both parties. The breeds must be assigned and approved. Now the judge must make his travel arrangements, hopefully far enough in advance to get a good-priced airfare. Traveling can be a stressful situation, but is justified by the fun

apply for additional breeds, based on the number of breeds for which he has already been approved, through the procedures described below.

Applying for additional breeds requires attendance at breed specialties, seminars and

and satisfaction realized at the other end of the journey.

The show-giving club will provide the judges with transportation, accommodations and several meals over the course of the weekend. What the judge should bring to wear will depend on whether it is an indoor or outdoor show, the time of the year and the location of the show. For example, if a judge lives in Florida and is going to judge a show in Colorado in November, he will have to bring heavy winter clothing and be prepared for the sudden and dramatic change in climate, temperature and elevation.

Above all, a judge must be flexible with all arrangements, environments, show sites, accommodations, etc., and still be pleasant and enjoy what he does during the day, which allows for the opportunity to see and judge many dogs, as well as visit with friends he may see only occasionally. A judge can always learn something new from his fellow judges. When it ceases to be enjoyable, then it is time to leave the judging arena.

PREPARING YOUR SHOW PUPPY

Exhibiting a dog to his championship starts back in the breeder's planning stages, before the puppy is even born. Which male dog is selected to breed to a given bitch is very important. The breeder wants to perpetuate and encourage the desirable points of each mate, according to the requirements of the breed standard, while eliminating any unsavory qualities. Each breed has an official written standard that depicts a detailed description, and thus visual image, of the ideal for that breed. The national breed club prepares the standard and obtains the club membership's approval, and then the AKC endorses the standard. A well-worded, detailed standard helps to clarify to breeders, exhibitors and judges how to visualize and recognize what is expected for the breed.

After selecting and mating the breeding pair, the puppies arrive! The breeder must be on his toes, making sure that mom and puppies stay healthy. Vaccinations are required for the puppies at the appropriate time, and, when they are around eight weeks old, the breeder looks at the pups with an eye toward show quality. Not all puppies in a litter are worthy of championship. The breeder continues to watch the puppies, and by 12 weeks of age it is time

AVAILABLE POINTS

It is quite possible that there will be no dogs entered in some of the classes, or only one or two dogs entered and shown. The fewer dogs entered, the fewer the available points toward championship.

for him to make the decision as to which are pet-quality and which are show-quality.

Puppies may be shown in AKC-licensed shows at six months of age, no earlier. However, training sessions called "matches," established by local dog clubs, can be a good way to expose puppies to the show-dog game. A puppy of any age that is current on his vaccinations, healthy and needs to be prepared for the show ring is qualified to enter a match. It is very important that this training time be presented as a fun thing for the two of you to do together. If you cause the puppy to become stressed by dragging him around the ring or babying him too much, you both may lose the spirit for all future endeavors.

Depending on the breed, the dog must be taught patience for grooming, whether it involves stripping, scissoring, brushing or merely "trim toenails and go." A dog cannot win if he doesn't show himself to his best advantage. The dog that gets in the ring and "asks" for the win may well be a lesser quality dog, but having a confident temperament and sparkling presence may diminish his faults; thus he could well be regarded more highly than the more correct dog with the lackluster personality. After all, the name of the sport is "showing." There must be a limit, of course, to the faults that will be accepted, to prevent the loss of breed type.

PROMOTING YOUR DOG

The American dog scene is a lucrative market for magazines, advertisements and dissemination of information about the canine goings-on in each state and throughout the country. There are several all-purpose, all-breed publications that encourage breeders and exhibitors to advertise their dogs' wins, their breeding successes and any other accomplishments. All magazines are sent free to group judges.

There are also breed and group magazines that offer the same opportunities. This is a matter of creating nationwide awareness of your dog's activities on the show scene. Does this affect the judge's

"Backstage" at a dog show, dogs are often crated while awaiting their time in the ring, and the handlers need a break, too.

decision? It should not. After all, someone may prefer chocolate and someone else may like vanilla. And on any given day, a dog may or may not perform to his maximum ability. If there are two equal-quality dogs in the ring, there can be other influences, such as breed, individual preferences for certain points, etc.

The spectators' applause, for the most part, is not even heard by the adjudicating official. All in all, AKC judging is non-prejudicial and unbiased, due to the intense education and study required for approval to judge a breed. The AKC is very insistent on a judge's thorough breed knowledge to enable him to correctly evaluate each dog.

PROFESSIONAL HANDLERS

When discussing dog shows, the "Land of the Free" has become the "Land of the Fee." The United States has become *the* nation of professional handlers. Most champions (or "specials") these days are presented (or exhibited) by professional handlers, and 90% of the dogs winning Best in Show every weekend have a professional paid suit on the human end of the leash. While the United Kennel Club, America's alternative registry does not permit professional handlers to compete in their shows, the AKC supports this aspect of the sport.

Are professional handlers bad for the sport of dog showing? The answer is a resounding "Yes" and

"No." Professional handlers in the US (and Canada, too) have elevated the playing field, making competition ever steeper and the quality of presentation and grooming superior to anywhere else in the world. Shows in England, for example, pale in comparison in terms of slickness and panache, as American dogs are groomed to the 9's and handler-presented as if they are on the runway. The best professional handlers make a career of conditioning, grooming and presenting dogs and they know their business well. Many of these professionals have been "in dogs" for their whole lives, having begun as Junior Handlers and raised by parents who

MAGAZINES FOR THE FANCY

All show people should subscribe to the two leading periodicals dedicated to the sport of pure-bred dogs, *Dog World* and *Dogs in Review*. Write to PO Box 6050, Mission Viejo, CA 92690-6050 for information about subscriptions or visit the staff at www.dogworldmag.com and www.dogsinreview.com. *Dog World*, established in 1916, is recognized as the authority on dogs and has won many awards for its articles on dog topics from health and grooming to flyball, breeding and legal issues. *Dogs in Review* is geared toward the serious dog fancier, including breeders, handlers and judges. Its global perspective and inclusion of dog-show activities worldwide make it unique among American conformation periodicals.

also are breeders, exhibitors and/or judges. We should not underplay the expertise required of these individuals. Proper care, presentation and conditioning require 24-7 commitment and hard work as well as knowledge and education.

Professional handlers are thoroughly experienced in how to present a dog to its advantage and can, on occasion, win over a more deserving dog who might be carelessly groomed, clumsily handled and/or not controlled. One would think that a judge can see through that illusion—and most can. However, not being totally knowledgeable in a particular breed could cause the judge to be swayed in the 'fancy' picture. It happens!

Dog owners interested in showing their dogs have to compete with these professionals in the ring, thus requiring the owner/exhibitor to learn more about showing dogs and become as competent as possible. To finish a Champion in an AKC show, much less campaign one, costs thousands of dollars, and who can compete with the owners who are paying high prices on a weekly basis to have their dog professionally exhibited? It could be disheartening to newcomers unless one is completely motivated to excel in the sport. Breeding a top winning dog is the most important, but having presented him to top wins is euphoric! It can and has, many times over, been done. This book, of course, is not about hiring a profes-

sional handler, but this may be an option for you; likewise, it may be your choice to become a professional handler or professional breeder/handler. If you can't beat 'em, join the PHA!

The Professional Handlers' Association (PHA) is the largest organization in the US dedicated to the sport of handling pure-bred dogs. The PHA aims to improve relationships between professional handlers and their clients, providing support to the handlers at shows and with the AKC. It also educates members through open forums, seminars, lectures and other such functions. Members are required to be active in the dog fancy for at least ten years as well as meet other rigid criteria. Contact the Professional Handlers' Association at 17017 Norbrook Drive, Onley, Maryland 20832. Canadian fanciers should contact the Canadian Professional Handlers' Association (CPHA) at 7542 Fifth Line, Milton, Ontario L9T 2X8.

The AKC offers a Registered Handlers Program, which is designed to establish criteria and standards for professional handlers. Members must fulfill certain criteria, including seven years experience in handling, and commit to a Code of Ethics. The AKC website includes the complete Code of Ethics, application and additional information and also lists the Registered Handlers state by state with short profiles of each handler.

ABOUT THE AUTHOR

Ann D. Hearn's first impressive moment with pure-bred dogs was in Washington, DC at the age of five years old. Her father, a government employee with the National Relief Agency (NRA) worked with members of the White House. Each year during Easter, the White House front lawn, a large open grassy area, was made available for an Easter egg hunt for the children, and Ann and her sister Nell were invited.

On one such Sunday, while scrambling for the eggs, President Franklin D. Roosevelt came out on the lawn and had Fala, his pure-bred Scottish Terrier, with him. Ann was fascinated and impressed with the temperament and looks of the delightful dog and his close attendance to the man in the wheelchair. From that point on, it became her goal to have that sort of joy and companionship in her life. On the first anniversary of her marriage, some 16 years later, her new husband gave her a Wire Fox Terrier puppy and the bond was established, to be enjoyed more and more each passing year.

Mrs. Hearn presently is an approved AKC judge for the Terrier, Toy and Non-Sporting Groups, Best in Show, Junior Showmanship and Miscellaneous Classes. She intends to further her career with application for additional breeds in the future. She has judged in Australia, Italy, South Africa, Russia, Finland, Canada and Hawaii. She lives in a suburb of Atlanta, Georgia with her husband.

Ch. Rise N Shine's Maine Chance, owned/bred by Lori Tuttle and April Geiseking, also owned by Barb Winans, winning Best in Specialty Show.

SHOWING IN BRITAIN

just one. It is only at these shows that dogs may compete for the coveted title of Champion, and the system in Britain is such that it is the most difficult country in the world for a dog to gain this title. This is primarily because all dogs effectively compete for the Challenge Certificate (CC), with the winners of each class competing against each other before the final decision is made. In the majority of cases, some of these dogs have already gained their championship

The Best in Show winner at Crufts in 2003, Pekingese Ch. Dangerous Liaison, pictured with judge Albert Wight and happy owner-handler Bert Easdon.

TYPES OF SHOWS

In Britain, there are various different types of shows under The Kennel Club system, each of which has something of its own character. First, I must stress that constant changes are made within the dog world, so what is true today may not necessarily be true tomorrow. However, any changes made by The Kennel Club, Britain's ruling body on pure-bred dogs and the sport, are always done with the dogs' best interests in mind.

At the very top of the scale are Championship Shows, which can be for all breeds, several breeds or

THE UK'S JUDGING SYSTEM

The system of judging in Britain is very different from that in the majority of countries, with the notable exception of Australia. For the last few years, The Kennel Club has had a Judge's Working Party, which has worked constantly to improve the show scene for all concerned. Although rules change, the changes are always publicized in the canine press, and various rulebooks can be obtained by requesting them from The Kennel Club. These books can also be purchased at The Kennel Club's stand at the Crufts show and at some major Championship Shows.

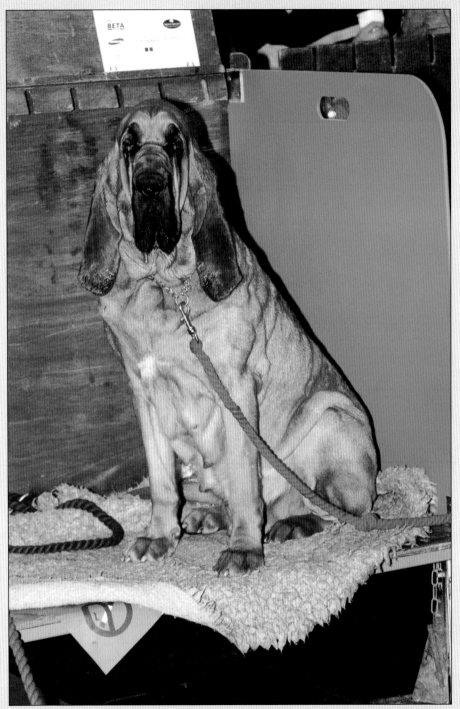

A Bloodhound in his benching area at Crufts. The Crufts show is the largest benched show in the UK, attracting over 20,000 entries.

England's top Airedale Terrier Ch. Jokyl This Is My Song was a Reserve BIS winner at Crufts.

titles, which makes competition very stiff indeed. To get past a top winner in your breed is no mean feat, particularly in the numerically strong breeds, in which entries can run into the hundreds.

To become a champion, a dog must be awarded three CCs, under three different judges, and at least one of these must be awarded after the age of 12 months. If the judge sees fit, he can award a CC and Reserve CC in each sex. In doing so, he is stating that, in his opinion, these dogs are worthy of the title of Champion. Reserve awards, though, do not count toward the title unless the CC is for some reason subsequently disallowed.

COLOR CONFUSION
The first-prize winner in Britain collects a red rosette and prize card. In the United States, red goes to the second-place winner, and it is the blue rosette that is awarded to the class winner. This difference in colors has led to some embarrassing situations for judges when judging away from home!

Once he has earned his championship, a dog can go on to win any number of CCs, but his title of Champion will always remain the same. The title is represented by the abbreviation Ch. in front of the dog's name. In gundog breeds and Border Collies, dogs are not

A day at a show is a long and exhausting one. These Alaskan Malamutes enjoy some well-deserved downtime in the benching area.

allowed to carry the full title of Champion in front of their names unless they have also qualified in Field Trials. Hence, most dogs in these breeds found in the show rings are Show Champions (Sh. Ch.), and those who have become full Champions can be deservedly proud.

At Championship Shows, many different classes are offered, some restricted by age, others by previous wins. Details of the classes are always printed in the schedule, which is available before the show.

General Championship Shows are now divided into seven groups: Hound, Pastoral, Terrier, Toy, Utility, Gundog and Working. After breed judging is complete, the Best of Breed winners compete for Best in Group, with first through fourth place being awarded. At the end of the show, which can last from two to four days, all seven of the group winners compete for Best in Show and Reserve Best in Show. At some Championship Shows, there is also a competition for Best Puppy in Show and Reserve Best Puppy in Show; this competition always is held at breed club events.

Various "Stakes" classes are also offered. These generally are either sponsored by a company or

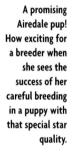

A promising Airedale pup! How exciting for a breeder when she sees the success of her careful breeding in a puppy with that special star quality.

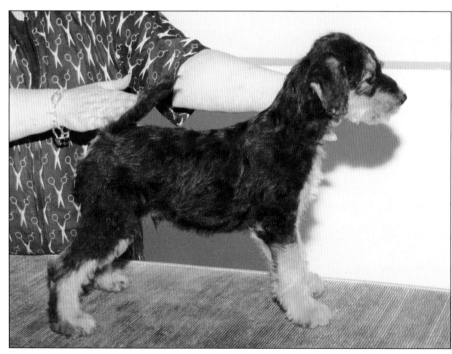

Ringside at a show, you can meet other dog enthusiasts and introduce spectators to your breed. It's fun and educational for all concerned, human and canine.

CRUFTS QUALIFIERS

The qualification for entry at Crufts is published in advance of the show each year. This is dependent upon specific wins in the preceding year, but a dog that has obtained a Kennel Club Stud Book Number by merit of his high achievement is eligible for entry at Crufts for life.

held in memory of a significant person who has done a great deal for the show-giving society.

One step down is the Open Show, in which the classifications can be much the same, but on a significantly smaller scale. Not all Open Shows are judged on the Group system; therefore, in some cases, all Best of Breed winners compete together for the title of Best in Show and Reserve. At Open Shows, young dogs of a certain age can gain points that count toward The Kennel Club's Junior Warrant (JW) title, entitling the dog to have JW added to his name, though such points also have to be gained at Championship Shows.

Limited Shows are few and far between these days. These shows must be limited in some way, usually to members of a given club or to people residing in a certain area. However, there may be alternative limitations as agreed upon by The Kennel Club.

For all three types of shows just described, entries have to be made well before the show date. Exemption Shows, however, are quite different and are entered on the day of the show. With Exemption Shows, the emphasis is on fun. There usually is a very restricted number of pedigree classes along with several "fun" classes, such as "dog with the waggiest tail" and the like. At such shows, funds can only be raised for a charity, and although the Kennel Club has to grant a license, both registered and unregistered dogs may enter. However, for Exemption and Limited Shows, dogs that have won Challenge Certificates, or any award that counts toward the title of Champion, are not eligible to compete.

Matches and Special Events are other types of competitive events, both of which have certain restrictions laid down by The Kennel Club. In a Match, often one club invites another for a small competition. Special Events are generally organized when winning dogs from throughout the year compete for an overall title.

ENTERING SHOWS IN BRITAIN

In Britain, all Championship, Open and Limited Shows are advertised in the weekly canine presses, and exhibitors need to contact the secretaries of the various clubs to ask for show schedules. In addition, breed clubs usually send out schedules to

Weighing a Miniature Dachshund before the show. In the UK, the standard states that "it is of the utmost importance that judges should not award prizes to animals over 5.0 kgs (11 lbs)" in the Miniature variety of the breed.

their members and, in most cases, societies automatically circulate schedules to those who exhibited at their previous events.

The schedules are fairly self-explanatory, but must be filled out carefully, in clearly legible writing. The costs of show entries vary, but the most expensive are General Championship Shows, where exhibitors are effectively covering the cost of enormous overheads, including benching, which is obligatory. This is generally in the region of £20 per dog, with a small extra fee if the dog is entered in more than one class. Breed club and Open Show entries are considerably less expensive, as dogs do not have to be benched and overheads are lower. The cost of Limited Show entry is rarely more than a couple of pounds or so. At Exemption Shows, the fee, payable on the day of the show, is very little indeed.

TO CONTACT THE KC
The Kennel Club
1-5 Clarges St., Piccadilly, London
W1Y 8AB, UK
www.the-kennel-club.org.uk

JUDGES' TRAINING AND QUALIFICATIONS
Training of judges in Britain has changed quite dramatically in recent years, and what The Kennel

WINNING THE TICKET

Earning a championship at Kennel Club shows is the most difficult in the world. Collecting three green tickets not only requires much time and effort, it can be very expensive! Challenge Certificates, as the tickets are properly known, are the building blocks of champions—good breeding, good handling, good training and good luck!

Club considers to be improvements are continually being made. Hitherto, progress up the ladder of success as a judge was largely by way of hands-on experience, but now seminar attendance and assessment are necessary as well. Breed clubs operate a system of "A," "B" and "C" judging lists according to people's judging experience, seminar attendance and, in some cases, examination success. Unfortunately, even when candidates meet all of the criteria, committees have an all-too-powerful role in making the final decision as to who and who should not be included.

Open and Limited Shows are considered training grounds for judges, but, sadly, opportunities for newer judges to pick up appointments at such shows are increasingly limited. In part, this is because the system has evolved whereby judges must be on a "B" list before they can judge a given number of classes for a breed. Another important factor is that, in order to judge variety classes or groups or to award Best in Show and Best Puppy in Show, a judge must award CCs in at least one breed. This results in CC judges being invited to judge a number of breeds, with variety classes and at least one group, meaning that there are few classes available for novice judges. Of course, not all societies operate in this way, but a high proportion of them do.

One of the main problems encountered by well-established British judges who are invited to officiate abroad is that although they probably have very substantial experience in judging breeds other than those in which they award CCs, they do not judge them at "championship level" in

In Junior Handling, dogs of all breeds can be seen in the ring, as it is the handler's presentation that counts. This little lady has this Great Dane completely under control, gaiting beautifully by her side.

the UK. In some cases, this is because certain breeds in Britain are simply not entitled by The Kennel Club to compete for the title of Champion. This can often preclude such people from assessing dogs in other countries, when in actuality they probably have considerably more experience than many judges from other countries who are entitled to award CACIBs (awards toward a Fédération Cynologique Internationale international championship) all over the world.

Judging at championship level means that a judge has been approved by The Kennel Club to award CCs in a particular breed. To gain such approval, a judge must have had several years of experience as a judge. Those now being passed by The Kennel Club for their first breed at this level must also pass an official examination on ring procedure and attend a Kennel Club seminar on

CHAMPIONSHIP REQUIREMENTS

Until 1950, any dog in Britain could earn the title of Champion by winning three Challenge Certificates. Today, the prestigious title of Champion requires that the dog win three tickets and qualify in the field. The Kennel Club introduced the title of Show Champion for the dog winning three tickets (but without a field qualification). A Dual Champion is a dog that has obtained the title of Show Champion as well as that of Field Trial Champion.

conformation and movement. Although it is The Kennel Club that makes the ultimate decision as to whether or not a judge can award CCs, breed clubs will be consulted as to a candidate's suitability; the person concerned will already have to have reached an "A" list. Each club within a breed sets down criteria for inclusion on the various lists, though these requirements inevitably will vary according to the numerical strength of the breed.

It is difficult to be specific about official assessment of new Championship Show judges, for things are in the process of change. Some judges are assessed as to their suitability to award CCs at their first such appointment;

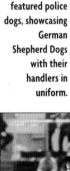

A special exhibit at Crufts featured police dogs, showcasing German Shepherd Dogs with their handlers in uniform.

> ## THE KC AND STANDARDS
> In the United States, breed standards are written and approved by the breed's parent club, then submitted to the AKC for approval. This is a complete departure from the way standards are handled in England, where all standards and changes are controlled by The Kennel Club.

others may be assessed under the new scheme, which involves three assessments beforehand. In all cases, Kennel Club approval to award CCs is only given for one appointment at a time, so even though a judge may have awarded CCs, this honor can indeed be taken away if there is good reason to do so. Judges who officiate for

variety classes, group and Best in Show competition at the championship level must award CCs in multiple breeds.

THE JUDGE'S JOB

It is a judge's job to assess the dogs before him and to place them in order of merit. At the close of each class, winners must be selected from first place downward, according to the number of place cards the society has elected to award. Usually this is four or five places at Open Shows, and five at Championship Shows, with more at the prestigious Crufts show, held annually. At all times, the dogs must be placed from left to right, and in descending order, unlike the system in most other countries. It is a Kennel Club rule that the first-prize winner is followed by the second, and so on.

In England, a judge usually writes a critique only on the first two placings in each class at Championship level, and for first-prize winners only at Open and Limited events. This, though, is only done roughly at the time, and is generally carefully typed up after the event and submitted to the canine press for publication. The newspapers *Our Dogs* and *Dog World* will only guarantee to publish reports that reach them within one month of the show date.

Judges must at all times conduct themselves in a proper manner and, strictly speaking,

KENNEL CLUB GROUPS

In the 1850s, there were just two divisions of all breeds: Sporting and Non-Sporting. The Kennel Club today divides its breeds into seven groups: Gundog, Utility*, Working, Toy, Terrier, Hound and Pastoral.*

*The Utility Group was established in 1968. The Pastoral Group, established in 1999, includes those sheepdog breeds previously categorized in the Working Group.

they should not comment on the dogs they are assessing until judging is complete. When awarding CCs in a breed, the Kennel Club

The judge goes down the line of Airedales, looking at each from the side in the stacked position.

Bulldogs are judged a little differently, positioned "head-on," and the judge walks around the dogs to evaluate them front and back.

restricts the number of dogs that may be judged on one day. If judging one breed, the maximum is 250; for two breeds, 200 and for three breeds, 120.

WHAT A STEWARD DOES

It is a steward's responsibility to assist the judge in his duties and to ensure the smooth and efficient running of the ring. However, it must be remembered that the judge is in control of the ring, not the steward, and that the steward should always follow the judge's directives.

Stewards may only allow into the ring the dogs that are entered in that specific class. They do not have the power to transfer dogs from one class to another or to allow unentered exhibits into the ring, except with authority from the appropriate official. It should also be noted that stewards do not have any authority over whether or not a dog is eligible to compete in a class.

A steward has to take care of paperwork, such as completing awards and posting them up for

An Italian Spinone gaits against the sweeping backdrop of the English countryside. What a location for an outdoor show, providing the spectators with breathtaking scenery and beautiful dogs.

exhibitors to see, as relevant. A steward must also take all reasonable steps to ensure that exhibitors are aware that judging is due to take place, and that each exhibitor is wearing the correct ring number.

These are only some of a steward's duties at a show. Full information about what stewarding comprises is published in The Kennel Club's *Guide For Stewards*.

For newer judges who hope one day to judge at championship level, stewarding is essential. It is a rule that the person must have carried out a certain number of stewarding appointments before applying for inclusion on a club's "A" judging list. This is a newer rule, though, and does not apply to those who had already awarded CCs before its enforcement.

PET PASSPORT

In the near future we are likely to see dogs from different countries competing more frequently and more freely with each other. The introduction of the "Pet Passport" enables dogs to travel abroad without having to go into quarantine upon their return to Britain.

The author, who specializes in Tibetan breeds, awards Best of Breed in Tibetan Mastiff judging.

ABOUT THE AUTHOR

Juliette Cunliffe, breeder, exhibitor and International Championship Show judge, has a wealth of experience in the world of dogs. Based in the UK, she has judged in many other countries throughout the world, traveling as far north as Scandinavia and Russia, and south to Australia.

Highly respected as one of the world's experts in Tibetan breeds, she also has special interest in all Oriental breeds and in Hounds, with sighthounds being a very important part of her life.

With high qualifications as both a judge and breeder, as an exhibitor she has owned Champion and Junior-Warrant-winning dogs. A Kennel-Club-Accredited Trainer, Juliette also lectures frequently on dogs, and is well known as a prolific author of well-researched books and a regular correspondent for canine newspapers and magazines.

Author Juliette Cunliffe awards the Dog CC to a Tibetan Terrier, her eventual Best in Show winner at a show in Australia.

The author awards Best in Show at Sweden's Tibethund show.

SHOWING IN EUROPE AND BEYOND

BY DR. ROBERT POLLET

MEET THE FCI

The Fédération Cynologique Internationale (FCI), established on May 22, 1911, is the "international canine federation." "Cynology" means literally "the science of dogs" and "the organized dog fancy or hobby." "Cynological" (in French, *cynologique*) is the adjectival form of "cynology" and can be replaced by the synonym "canine."

The FCI was created with the aim of promoting and protecting cynology and pure-bred dogs. The FCI's founding nations are Germany, Austria, Belgium, France and the Netherlands. World War I brought an end to this federation; however, it was recreated in 1921 by the governing canine organizations of France and Belgium, which drew up its new by-laws. The office of the FCI is still located in Thuin, Belgium.

The FCI is composed of 80 member countries and contract partners that each issue their own pedigrees and train their own judges. The FCI recognizes about 330 breeds. This is practically double the amount of breeds recognized by any other country or kennel club. Each of these breeds is considered the "property" of a specific country. The "owner" countries write the breed standards of their national breeds in cooperation with the Standards and Scientific Commissions of the FCI. FCI breed standards are published in the four official languages of the FCI (English, French, German and Spanish). The pedigrees and the judges are mutually recognized by all of the FCI member countries.

FCI SHOWS

ESSENTIAL DIFFERENCES FROM AKC AND KENNEL CLUB SHOWS

The FCI, just like the AKC, England's Kennel Club and other canine organizations (Canadian Kennel Club, Australian National Kennel Council, etc.), governs conformation shows (sometimes called "beauty shows" by exhibitors). The FCI furnishes the rules and regulations for the International Shows. Regarding National Shows, the member countries of the FCI have their own rules, which are similar to each other but not identical, and

The French Bulldog is a charming breed known around the world. This handsome representative of the breed poses with his trophy, won in an FCI competition.

A charming pair of Lagotta Romagnola, relaxing at ringside.

many points a dog earns by winning at a given show and depending on how many dogs are defeated. A dog doesn't win points; rather, he earns Certificates. The number of entries or dogs defeated has no bearing on earning a Certificate. Other basic differences (judging system, ring technique, etc.) will be mentioned later in the chapter.

TYPES OF SHOWS

The FCI and/or its member countries govern many different types of shows. The most prestigious, which are all-breed shows, are the World Dog Show, hosted in a different country each year; the Section Dog Shows (e.g., the European Dog Show) and the International Championship Shows, where a dog can earn the titles of World or European Champion or the CACIB certificate.

The CACIB (*Certificat d'Aptitude au Championnat International de Beauté*) and the CAC (*Certificat d'Aptitude au Championnat National de Beauté*) are, respectively, the International and the National Certificates of the FCI. At International Championship Shows, both the CACIB and CAC certificates can be won.

At the national level, we can distinguish the following types of shows:
• All-breed Shows with CAC, run by general canine societies, where

which may not conflict with the general guidelines or regulations of the FCI.

Exhibitors who are used to AKC and Kennel Club Shows will notice the following differences when they participate in International and/or National Shows held under the auspices of the FCI:

• Judging is done more slowly; the number of entries for a judge seldom exceeds more than 90 dogs;

• Each dog is given an individual written detailed critique, called a "judge report," which in essence is a description of the dog's conformation and movement. The judge dictates this critique to the ring secretary;

• Each dog is given a rating or quality grading, called a "qualification," based solely on conformation to the breed standard;

• Champion titles can only be won by earning Certificates. There is no system to determine how

been a successful exhibitor for at least five years, or have been actively involved in canine matters for at least five years.
• Have been on duty at official shows as a ring steward or secretary (at least five times).
• Have been examined in writing on the following subjects: anatomy, morphology and movement of dogs; genetics, health and character; knowledge of the breed standard; techniques of judging; national regulations and FCI Show regulations for International Shows.
• Having had practical training (breed knowledge, show regulations, judging procedure, ring control, etc.) and practical education (judging dogs and writing reports) under the supervision of FCI show judges.

JUDGE REPORTS (CRITIQUES)

At FCI shows, dogs shown are given individual written judge reports or critiques, and are then given quality gradings (qualifications). This system involves much work on the part of the judges and the ring staff, but it has the great advantage that every exhibitor gets the judge's actual opinion about and impression of his dog.

The individual critique, which the judge dictates to the ring secretary, includes an overall assessment of the dog, covering the dog's main merits and faults.

At the conclusion of the breed judging, a copy of the critique is given to the exhibitor.

Dictating reports is not easy. Some reports are very short, others are more complete; some are rather vague, others very instructive. The critique should always make clear why the specific qualification, mentioned at the end of the critique, was awarded. Likewise, the reason for a "Disqualified" or a "Cannot be judged" should be given if one of these gradings has been given.

The Picardy Shepherd, or Berger Picard, is one of the oldest French sheepherders, named after France's Picardy region. What a sweet-looking breed!

Akita (Great Japanese Dog) "Spike" at an FCI show hosted by the Kennel Club of Chile. Spike went BOB, Group 1 and fourth-place overall in the show.

(complete or not, missing teeth, bite); eyes (shape, set, color); ears (set-on, shape, size); neck; forequarters (length and layback of shoulder and upper arm, angulation, forefeet, positions); withers; back, loin and croup; depth and width of chest; underline and belly; hindquarters (length of upper and lower thigh, angulation, hindfeet, positions); tail (set-on, length, carriage); coat (color, texture, condition, undercoat); movement (rear drive, back transmission, reach of stride) and character. Of course, when making his assessment and remarks, the judge must always take into consideration the requirements of the standard for the breed that he is judging.

The reports should not be too general. They should provide information to the exhibitor for educational purposes. For example, the judge is advised, when he mentions that the head is "nice" or "excellent," to include additional details such as "well-chiseled," "good length of muzzle," "good parallelism between forehead and muzzle," etc.

In the ideal, but not-always-seen, case of a truly complete report, the following points would be mentioned, in a logical order from head to tail, ending with remarks on the coat, gait and character: general appearance, including proportions (length of body) and sex character; head (strength, shape, skull, nose, muzzle); dentition

GRADING SYSTEM AND PLACEMENTS

As well as a detailed written critique, each dog is given a quality grading, known most commonly as a "qualification"

CREATING FCI STANDARDS

Each breed standard is a cooperative effort between the breed's "owner" country and the FCI's Standards and Scientific Commissions. Judges use these official breed standards at shows held in FCI member countries. One of the functions of the FCI is to update and translate the breed standards into French, English, Spanish and German.

(also called a "grading" or "rating"). The qualifications can be defined as follows:

• Excellent (Exc.): awarded to dogs that come very close to the ideal dog, as detailed in the breed standard, which are shown in excellent condition, display harmonious, well-balanced temperaments, are of high quality and have brilliant posture. Their superior characteristics in respect to their breed permit that minor imperfections can be ignored. They should, however, have the typical features of their sex. Only Excellent dogs may receive a Championship Certificate.

• Very Good (VG): may only be awarded to dogs that possess the characteristic qualities of their breed, have well-balanced proportions and are in correct condition. A few minor faults may be tolerated, but none of a morphological nature. This grading can only be granted to dogs of high quality. Very Good dogs may receive a first place in their class but not a Championship Certificate.

• Good (G): to be awarded to dogs that possess the characteristics of the breed, even if showing faults, provided that these are not concealed.

• Sufficient (Suff.) or Satisfactory: to be awarded to dogs that correspond adequately to their breed, without possessing the generally accepted characteristics, or whose

FCI GROUPS

Following are the names of the ten official groups. The official FCI list of all breeds indicates if each breed is entitled to CACIBs and if the breed needs a Working Trial to earn the CACIB title.

Group I: Sheepdogs and Cattle Dogs (except Swiss Cattle Dogs);
Group II: Pinschers, Schnauzers, Mastiffs (Molossians) and Swiss Mountain and Cattle Dogs;
Group III: Terriers;
Group IV: Dachshunds (Teckels);
Group V: Spitzes and primitive-type dogs;
Group VI: Scenthounds and related breeds;
Group VII: Pointers;
Group VIII: Retrievers, Flushing Dogs and Water Dogs;
Group IX: Companion and Toy Dogs;
Group X: Sighthounds (Windhounds)

physical condition leaves something to be desired.

• Disqualified: should be given to dogs atypical of their breed, bad-tempered, aggressive or having a disqualifying fault (with respect to testicles, dentition, coat length or color, size, etc.) as specified in the breed standard.

• Cannot be judged: to be given to dogs that do not move or that jump constantly, try to get out of the ring or avoid being examined by the judge. The same grading applies if the judge suspects faking (operations or treatments to change the dog's appearance, with

At a show in the Netherlands, the Bullmastiff, Tibetan Mastiff and Pug stand atop the winners' platform.

which are not official qualifications, are Very Promising, Promising, Satisfactory and Not Promising.

In some countries (such as those in Scandinavia), the grading terminology is somewhat different. Instead of Exc., VG, G and Suff., the gradings of first (typical and correct in conformation), second (a good dog without outstanding faults), third (a dog with obvious faults, but still acceptable type) or 0 (an atypical, bad-tempered or nervous dog, or one having a disqualifying fault) are used to indicate the quality of exhibits. In these countries, a "Champion Quality" grade can be given to the first-prize dogs of superior quality, and only these dogs compete for the National or International Championship Certificates.

THE BEAUTY CHAMPIONSHIP CERTIFICATES

In shows held under the auspices of the FCI, a dog of a recognized

the object to deceive, i.e., cover up or artificially correct faults). The reason for this rating must be included in the judge's report.

The top four dogs in each class are given placements of first through fourth place, with their qualification preceding their placement. Thus, if the top three dogs were qualified Exc., and the fourth-place dog was qualified VG, their placements would be Exc. 1, Exc. 2, Exc. 3 and VG 4. Dogs rated Good or below will not receive a placement. Thus if the top dog is rated Exc., the next two dogs VG and the fourth dog G, the placements would be Exc.1, VG 2 and VG 3; there would be no fourth place awarded. However, in some countries, placing of a Good dog is allowed.

In the Puppy Classes (from 6 to 9 months old), the ratings,

TYPES OF JUDGES

The designation of Show Judge is further broken down as follows:

• Breed Judge: has been approved to judge one or more breed(s);

• Group Judge: has been approved to judge one or more of the FCI official groups;

• Allrounder: has been approved to judge all breeds of the ten FCI recognized groups.

breed, male or female, can earn a National Beauty Certificate (*Certificat d'Aptitude au Championnat National de Beauté*, CAC) or an International Beauty Certificate (*Certificat d'Aptitude au Championnat International de Beauté*, CACIB). As signified by the French wording *Certificat d'Aptitude* ("aptitude certificate"), the FCI Certificate is not a full or definitive Champion title. The CACIB Certificates also are only "proposals to a CACIB," because the definitive awarding of the certificate has to be approved or validated by the FCI.

The CACIB Certificate is given to the best dog of the Intermediate, Open, Working and Champion Class, but only if he is of superior quality. The full title of International Beauty Champion can be awarded when the dog of a breed that is not subjected to work or hunting trials has won four International Certificates (CACIBs) in three different countries, under three different judges. One CACIB must be won in the dog's country of residence or the country of origin. For breeds that are subjected to work or hunting trials, two CACIBs and one Working or Hunting Certificate are required for the title.

The awarding of National Certificates (CACs) is effected according to the rules and regulations of the national canine organization (kennel club) where the show is held. In some countries, not only dogs in the Open, Working and Champion Classes but also dogs in the Junior and/or Veteran Classes compete for the National Certificate. However, in several countries, the Champion Class dogs do not compete for the CAC.

To gain the full title of National Beauty Champion, a dog or a bitch must earn two, three or four CACs; each country has its own requirements. As with the international title, the breeds that are subjected to work or hunting

MAXED OUT
The number of dogs assigned to a judge in one day may not exceed 80 if critiques are required; the maximum is 150 when no critiques are required.

trials need one Working or Hunting Certificate to become a National Champion. For the definitive National or International Champion title, there must be more than one year between the first and the last CAC or CACIB received.

Reserve CACs and Reserve CACIBs are given to the second-best dogs from all the classes in which the titles can be awarded. In some countries, there are no Reserve Certificates. All titles, CACs, CACIBs and Reserve Championship Certificates are given to dogs as well as bitches.

The World Dog Show attracts many working and hunting dogs as well as top show dogs. This handsome Bruno de Jura came from Switzerland to participate.

Club Shows, Specialty Shows or other types of shows.

At World Shows or Section Shows (e.g., the European Championship Show), the full and definitive title of World Winner or Section Winner (e.g., European Winner) is awarded to the dog and bitch that are proposed for the CACIB, irrespective of the number of entries for their particular breeds. At these shows, the title of World Junior Winner or Section Junior Winner (e.g., European Junior Winner) is awarded to the best young dog and bitch, provided that they have received the Excellent grading.

RING AND JUDGING PROCEDURE

JUDGING OF THE INDIVIDUAL CLASSES The procedure in the show ring can differ from judge to judge,

CACs or CACIBs (and the Reserves) can only be awarded to dogs that were given the Excellent grading. The judge is not obliged to give the title to an Excellent dog, because the dog should also be an "excellent dog of superior quality" or "of championship caliber." If not, the title (and also the Reserve title) can and should be withheld. In some countries, an Excellent dog is simply supposed to be of championship quality and the title may not be withheld. In other countries (such as Scandinavian), a "Champion Quality" grade (awarded to the best first-prize dogs) exists and is needed to receive the Certificate.

Special titles, such as Junior Winner, Winner, Club Champion, etc., can also be awarded at National or International Shows,

---

FCI FUNCTIONS

The FCI *does not* issue pedigrees. The FCI members and contract partners are responsible for issuing pedigrees and training judges in their own countries. The FCI does maintain a list of judges and makes sure that they are recognized throughout the FCI member countries.

The FCI also *does not* act as a breeder referral; breeder information is available from FCI-recognized national canine societies in each of the FCI's member countries.

BEYOND COMPARE

The FCI grading system in fact signifies and makes it clear that each dog is compared against the breed standard, not compared to the dog in front or behind him in the ring. So, in a particular class of dogs, it is quite possible that they all are Exc. or VG, or even that there are no Exc.- or VG-rated dogs at all.

from country to country and also from show to show (International, National, Specialty or Breed Show, Club Show, etc.). We can try, however, to describe here a general procedure, used at most FCI shows, as well as point out how FCI procedure differs from that of kennel clubs outside continental Europe.

Normally the judge is assisted by a ring staff, consisting of at least one steward and/or ring secretary. The ring steward helps the judge in implementing the desired ring procedure. He assembles the classes, checks the absentees and follows all of the judge's instructions. The ring staff usually consists of a ring secretary, who writes the critiques, and a ring steward. Sometimes (such as in the Netherlands) there is a third person who assists with the administrative work and distribution of the awards.

Dogs always compete before bitches (except in Puppy Classes). The classes are usually judged in the following order: Puppy, Junior, Intermediate, Open, Working, Champion and Veteran. The FCI demands that each dog in the class be judged with the same attention. The judge should always follow the same procedure when examining each dog. No exhibitor must feel slighted.

Perhaps you are now wondering, "What should an exhibitor know when he/she participates at FCI shows? What will I be required to do and how should I act in the ring?" You should be somewhat acquainted with FCI ring procedure, which is explained here.

Upon arrival, you should get your catalog, look for your ring, and pick up your entry (armband) number(s), which will be at either your bench or your breed's ring.

Great Dane, winning Best Non-Sporting Puppy at the Sydney Royal Championship Show in Australia. Australia is an FCI member country, but the Australian National Kennel Council group classifications differ a bit.

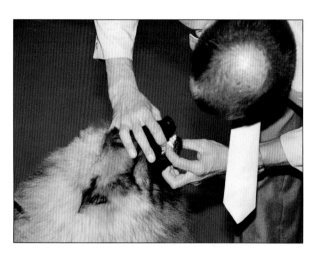

The judge checks the teeth and mouth of a German Wolfspitz.

Determine or ask how long you have before your class is judged. Do not use the general formula of "two minutes per entry," because the judge has to critique and qualify each dog. Plan on about three to five minutes per dog, but watch carefully, because this is only an estimate.

When your class is called, enter the ring. The ring steward will place the dogs in catalog order. It's very important to make your dog look good at this point, because most judges are already watching the dogs. At this moment, it's a great advantage if your dog displays a confident attitude. Your dog should walk into the ring with an air of "Here I am, look at me, I am beautiful!" Sometimes, when dogs are in the ring and the class is ready, the judge has all of the dogs gait around the ring as a class. This gives the judge a general impression of the quality of the class. Sometimes, especially at Breed or Specialty Shows, the judge will also approach each dog in turn to check the teeth and, with the males, the testicles.

Next, one at a time and in catalog (armband number) order, each dog is brought to the place that the judge or ring steward has indicated for individual examination. The judge checks the dog's mouth and, if a male dog, the testicles. First, you will show the bite by lifting up the dog's lips while his mouth is shut. The judge examines the front teeth, the smaller premolars on either side and sometimes, especially in working breeds, the large molars behind. He also checks the mouth pigmentation. The judge will appreciate it if you show the mouth with minimal fuss. If not, he will himself check the teeth and mouth.

Next, you will "stack" or "stand" your dog, which means that you "pose" him for the judge to view. Many judges do not want you to physically manipulate the dog's position. In some standards for working breeds, it is mentioned explicitly that the dog "is to be judged in its natural stance, without physical contact with the

CONTACT THE FCI
Fédération Cynologique Internationale
14, rue Leopold II, B-6530
Thuin, Belgium
www.fci.be

handler." The judge then views your dog from a distance and from different angles, and starts dictating his critique. When examining the dogs individually, especially those of the working breeds, FCI judges usually touch the dogs very little, and do not raise and drop the front or the rear or apply pressure on the back.

Although "double handling" (people outside the ring calling or making noises) is not allowed, there is for some breeds (e.g., German Shepherd Dogs!) and in some countries a certain tolerance with respect to the practice of attracting attention from outside the ring.

After having viewed your dog in show stance, the judge is ready to proceed to evaluating the dog's movement. He will ask you to gait your dog. Although a professional handler can hide a dog's faults, these usually become noticeable as the dog is gaited. As directed by the judge, you will first move the dog up and down in a straight line, and then you will be asked to let your dog trot once (perhaps two times) around the ring. Instead of an "up and down" movement, a "triangle" pattern is also common. After having moved your dog, you will be asked, after the judge has finished his critique, to go to the end of the line to wait. It is very important to know that most judges want all dogs to stay in the ring during the judg-

DRESS FOR THE OCCASION
At European dog shows, most exhibitors will be dressed casually. There are few professional handlers, although they are noticeably on the increase in some FCI countries.

ment of the entire class. Few exhibitors realize that most FCI judges, even while judging each dog individually in stance, are constantly but very rapidly looking around at the dogs waiting in line. This way, the judge is constantly evaluating the dogs in their natural posture, which can be very revealing and helpful when it's time to decide on the final placings.

When the individual evaluations are complete, the judge will finalize his decisions regarding placements. It is possible, after he has critiqued all dogs in the class, that he will ask all of the exhibitors to move their dogs in a circle around the ring and then put the four best dogs in placement order. Or it may be that all exhibitors are asked to put their dogs in show stance for the judge to give them all a final evaluation before they are placed. The judge clearly indicates the placements to the exhibitors and puts the four dogs to be placed in order of merit, in front of boards in the ring that are numbered from one to four.

While awarding placements or qualifications, especially at Specialty Shows, the judge may provide (although it is not required) verbal explanations to the exhibitors and/or public regarding the order of the placements or quality gradings. The critiques will be handed out at the end of the breed judging.

Awarding CACIBs, CACs, Reserves, Best of Breed, Best of Group and Best in Show

In all FCI countries, the same procedure applies for awarding the CACIB and the Reserve CACIB. As soon as all of the male classes have been judged, the dogs of the Intermediate, Open, Working and Champion Classes that have been placed Excellent first (first place in his class with an Excellent qualification) are called into the ring. The CACIB will be awarded to the best of these four dogs if he is of superior quality. The three other Excellent first dogs stay in the ring, and the Excellent second (second-place) dog of the class in which the CACIB was awarded is called into the ring. The Reserve CACIB will then be awarded to one of these four dogs (the three Excellent first dogs and the one Excellent second dog). The same process is repeated after all of the female classes have been judged.

This procedure, first the males and then the females, also applies for awarding the National Certificates (CAC and Reserve CAC), with the difference that, in some countries (the National Show rules are not the same in every country), the best dogs (if graded Excellent) of the Junior or even the Veteran class compete for the national title. So it is possible that the CAC is awarded not to the CACIB dog but to another dog (e.g., of the Junior Class) of still higher quality. Also, do not forget that in many countries the CAC cannot be awarded to a dog of the Champion Class. In still other countries, the CAC and CACIB must be given to the same dogs.

After having awarded the CACIB, CAC and Reserve titles, the judge has to choose the Best Dog and the Best Bitch. Out of these two, one is selected as Best of Breed and the other automatically is the Best of Opposite Sex. The Best Dog and the Best Bitch (if graded Excellent) of the Junior Class and, in some countries, even the best (if Excellent) of the Veteran Class also compete for the Best Dog, Best Bitch and Best of Breed titles.

The Best of Breed dogs are sent to the "ring of honor" for the finals. They all compete for the Best of Group title, together with all Best of Breed dogs that belong to the same FCI Group. The Best Puppy (graded Very Promising), the Best Veteran (if Excellent) and sometimes the Best of the Working Class (if Excellent) of each breed are also sent to the ring of honor, where they compete, with all of the other breeds, for Best in Show puppy and Best Veteran or Working Class dog.

Also during the finals, in the ring of honor, the Best Breeders' and the Best Progeny Group of each breed compete for the Best Breeders' Group in Show and the Best Progeny Group in Show. A Breeders' Group consists of a minimum of three dogs of the same kennel. The Progeny Group

consists of a stud dog or a brood bitch and at least four of their progeny, which may be from different litters.

Finally, the winners of the ten FCI groups (the ten Best of Group dogs) compete for Best in Show. The three best dogs should be placed, but very often the judge is asked to place all ten Best of Group dogs in order of quality.

A young exhibitor with a Braque Français (French pointing dog) of the Gascogne type at the World Dog Show.

Basenjis and handler winning Best Team in Show at the World Dog Show in Amsterdam.

critiques and, moreover, a grade or qualification should have value. However, sometimes even the highest grade (Excellent) seems to have little value. As a matter of fact, it happens that, in some countries and under some judges, in "open classes" with 50 to 60 entries, almost all of the exhibits, except two or three, are awarded the Excellent grade. If this becomes very commonplace, it would indeed be best to put an end to the grading system. While most exhibitors are quite happy when an Excellent grading has been given to almost every dog, these exhibitors have to realize that, in fact, most of them have been given illusions.

We also hear judges too often complaining about the exhibitors for whom a qualification of Very Good is looked upon as "bad." Exhibitors tend to think that, when a judge dares to give a Good grading, he must suffer from senility!

As to the judge reports, it is evident that, when describing a dog, the correct and appropriate canine terms should be used and that the exhibitors should be able to understand this specific canine terminology. Of course, dictating good judge reports is not easy at all; it supposes a thorough knowledge of the breed and perhaps also some literary talent. It once was written in a canine magazine that, if the practice of writing or

QUESTIONS AND CONTROVERSY

Very often in the FCI countries, the necessity or usefulness of the judge reports (critiques) and quality gradings (qualifications) are questioned. Sometimes the exhibitors wonder, especially when they are unhappy with the results, "Why not put an end to written critiques and qualifications? In other words, why not adopt the AKC or Kennel Club system?"

As already mentioned, the qualifications that are given to the dogs should be justified in the dictating judge reports was discontinued, a great advantage would be that "the requirements to become a Conformation Show Dog judge could be lowered by several levels, because everybody having a reasonable canine eye is able to designate the best dog in each class!"

Judge reports rather often cause problems because the exhibitors often either do not agree with the description of their dogs or remark that the day's description doesn't agree at all with prior critiques of the dog, either by different judges or by the same judge.

Nevertheless, it doesn't seem that the system of writing or dictating judge reports is going to disappear in the near future. An ideal situation would be that judge reports would be mandatory in all FCI countries (this is not the case at the moment), that there be a reasonable agreement between the reports of different judges on the same dogs and that, of course, the judges are well acquainted with canine terminology and the exhibitors are familiar with the terms used in judge reports. In any case, a written critique has great advantages and can be very educational, as the exhibitor gets the judge's actual opinion of his dog on that day. Therefore newer exhibitors will quickly learn about their dogs' shortcomings as well as virtues. The grading system

also can be rightly defended by arguing that in the United States or the United Kingdom a judge may leave a dog out of the placings, which, under a grading system, would have achieved an Excellent qualification.

In the FCI's new show regulations and the guidelines that serve as the basis for judging, it still is specified that the judge has to dictate an individual quality report for each dog and has to award a qualification. So we can conclude that, in spite of their questionability, the written critiques and the quality grades will not disappear soon.

Handler in traditional clothing with a pair of Polish Owczarek Podhalanski, a rare breed that you are only likely to find at a larger FCI show or a show in the breed's homeland.

Pictured at the World Dog Show in Amsterdam, judge Dr. Robert Pollet with owner Mrs. Bodil Rüsz of Denmark and Int. Ch. Napfényvárosi Csahos Jóság, a Group-2- and RBIS-winning Puli.

At an International Championship show in Luxembourg, the author and owner Loken Vigdis of Norway with the Group 2 and BIS winner, Int. Ch. Min Vesle-Frikk av Millcreek, a Bernese Mountain Dog.

PHOTO BY KARL DONVIL

ABOUT THE AUTHOR

Dr. Robert Pollet has been judging dogs since 1974. He is licensed to judge all breeds in the FCI's Group 1 (Sheepdogs and Cattledogs), Group 2 (Pinschers, Schnauzers, Molossians, etc.) and Group 5 (Spitz and primitive-type), as well as several other breeds. He is an ardent promoter of all Belgian breeds, especially Belgian Shepherd Dogs. He has vast judging experience with National, International and Specialty Shows. He has officiated at major shows in 21 European countries. He has judged Belgian Shepherds at all of the major shows in Europe, including the European Championship Show, World Dog Show, Crufts and FCI Supreme World Champion of Champions Show.

Dr. Pollet has been the president of the Belgian Committee for Nomination of Judges and is currently the delegate to the Judges Commission and the Show Commission of the FCI. He is president of the Belgian Shepherd Dog Club of the Transvaal (South Africa) and an honorary president of several dog clubs in Belgium.

Dr. Pollet is the author of many articles and books on dogs, including breed books on the Belgian Shepherd and the Schipperke. His study, *A Blueprint of the Belgian Shepherd Dog*, considered by breed fanciers as the definitive work on the breed, has been translated into eight languages.

His special interests are judging working dogs and the scientific aspects of the dog fancy, including genetics, anatomy, nutrition and dog behavior.

INDEX

Kennel Club Books™

The pet-book authority, Kennel Club Books is currently producing the

WORLD'S LARGEST SERIES OF DOG-BREED BOOKS,

including individual titles on 377 different dog breeds, representing every American Kennel Club recognized breed as well as hundreds of other rare breeds for which no title currently exists in English.

Each Kennel Club Breed Book is at least 158 pages, completely illustrated in color, with a hard-bound cover. The prestigious roster of authors includes world authorities in their breeds, as well as famous breeders, veterinarians, artists and trainers.

Explore the world of dogs by visiting kennelclubbooks.com on the Web and find out more about available titles on fascinating pure-bred dogs from around the globe.

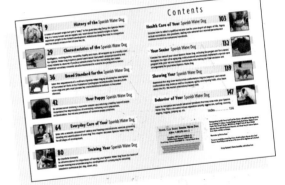

Kennel Club Books, LLC
308 Main Street, Allenhurst, NJ 07711 USA
(732) 531-1995 • www.kennelclubbooks.com